LEGENDS OF WARFARE

NAVAL

USS Nimitz (CVN-68)

America's Supercarrier: 1975 to the Present

SÉRGIO SANTANA

SCHIFFER MILITARY

4880 Lower Valley Road ■ Atglen, PA 19310

Designed by Justin Watkinson
Type set in Impact/Minion Pro/Univers LT Std

ISBN: 978-0-7643-5849-4
Printed in China

Published by Schiffer Publishing, Ltd.
4880 Lower Valley Road
Atglen, PA 19310
Phone: (610) 593-1777; Fax: (610) 593-2002
E-mail: Info@schifferbooks.com
www.schifferbooks.com

For our complete selection of fine books on this and related subjects, please visit our website at www.schifferbooks.com. You may also write for a free catalog.

Schiffer Publishing's titles are available at special discounts for bulk purchases for sales promotions or premiums. Special editions, including personalized covers, corporate imprints, and excerpts, can be created in large quantities for special needs. For more information, contact the publisher.

We are always looking for people to write books on new and related subjects. If you have an idea for a book, please contact us at proposals@schifferbooks.com.

Acknowledgments

This volume, intended to be the most updated account on the USS *Nimitz*, would not be possible without the invaluable and patient help provided by the following people: Éverton Pedroza, a longtime friend, graduated product designer, and skilled artist, who drew the set of artworks in this book; Anderson Subtil, another skilled artist and also a friend; Alexandre Galante (another longtime friend and retired Brazilian navy sailor); and Robinson Farinazzo Casal (Brazilian navy / marine corps commander, reserve), for their continuous support. BRAVO ZULU! Ensign Meagan Morrison, assistant public affairs officer / Media Division officer, USS *Nimitz* (CVN-68), for her prompt response in redirecting my request to some superior US Navy commands; Mark Aldrich, archivist and historian at Tailhook Association, for having made the association's files available to my work; LCdr. Lauren Cole, director of the Navy Office of Information East, for having provided the best possible assistance to this book; and Jonathan M. Roscoe, archivist, and Dave Colamaria, photo archivist, at Naval History and Heritage Command–Photo Section, for having provided high-resolution photographs published in this book. Special thanks to Robert Biondi, Schiffer senior editor, and Carey Massimini, Schiffer senior coordinator, for their full and patient support—a big thank you!

Contents

This book is dedicated to all those who served aboard the USS *Nimitz* since this unrivaled ship entered into service.

CHAPTER 1
Design, Construction, and Features

The *Nimitz* keel ceremony plaque. *US Navy*

Technically, the *Nimitz* carrier class came into being in February 1966, when Defense Secretary Robert Strange McNamara (1916–2009) approved the formation of a carrier force composed by fifteen vessels equipped with twelve wings. Of those, four would be nuclear powered (augmented by the CVAN-65 *Enterprise*, launched five years earlier). Under the same procurement plan, the three new ships were originally scheduled to be built every two years: the first vessel, CVAN-68, would be completed in 1971, funded by the fiscal year 1967 defense budget. However, its completion was delayed for four years.

The catalyst for McNamara's decision was the performance achieved by conventional aircraft carriers during the Vietnam War, then in progress. The three aircraft carriers would be built according to the US Navy Ship Characteristic Board 250 (SCB 250) standard. Later known as SCB 102, that standard prescribed features such as internal volume sufficient to hold 2.6 million gallons of JP-5 (which assured flight operations to be maintained for sixteen days, plus enough fuel for the escort ships) and 2,960 tons of aviation ordnance, all thanks to a 20-foot increase in the waterline length. The resulting aircraft carrier was to be powered by two nuclear reactors. Four C13-1 catapults were added.

The first of those ships was to honor the memory of US Navy fleet admiral Chester William Nimitz Sr. (1885–1966), a highly decorated officer who played a decisive role in the naval history of World War II as commander in chief of the US Pacific Fleet and the Pacific Ocean Areas, commanding Allied air, land, and sea forces during World War II.

The USS *Nimitz* keel was laid down on June 22, 1968, at Newport News Shipbuilding and Dry Dock Company, Virginia, in an event witnessed by Adm. Hyman Rickover, known as the "Father of the Nuclear Navy" for his role in the development of the nuclear propulsion for the US Navy.

A *Nimitz* bust ahead of the ship's frontal section. *US Navy*

A shipbuilder working in the USS *Nimitz*. *US Navy*

The US Navy band played when the *Nimitz* keel was laid on June 22, 1968, at Newport News, Virginia. *US Navy*

A worker involved in the *Nimitz* construction during his relaxation time. *US Navy*

Workers during the *Nimitz* construction process. *US Navy*

The *Nimitz* keel. *US Navy*

The keel of the *Nimitz* is lowered into the shipyard dock in Norfolk on June 22, 1968. *US Navy photo provided by USS* Nimitz *photo archives/Chief Petty Officer Porter Anderson*

A frontal view of the *Nimitz* prior to its launching ceremony. *US Navy*

Nimitz during its launching ceremony. *US Navy*

A truck is launched during the *Nimitz* catapult evaluation process.

The *Nimitz* performs a turn during sea trials. *US Navy*

The *Nimitz* arrives at Pier 12 in Norfolk, after official delivery to the Navy. *US Navy*

A CH-46 Sea Knight helicopter replenishes the *Nimitz* for its first cruise. *US Navy*

Another shot of the same helicopter. *US Navy*

Artist's conception of the future USS *Nimitz* (CVAN-68), May 1967. *US Navy*

Finally, after almost four years of construction and many trials, the USS *Nimitz* was christened on May 13, 1972, by Mrs. Catherine Nimitz Lay, Adm. Nimitz's widow. Gerald R. Ford, the president of the United States by then, commanded the ceremony.

On June 30 of that year, Capt. Bryan W. Compton was appointed as the USS *Nimitz*'s first commanding officer. In March 1975, the new ship went full nuclear power, faced builder's training and government.

In structural terms, the USS *Nimitz* is divided into external and internal sections. The former comprises the flight deck and carrier's island structure. The CVN's flight deck measures 1,092 feet by 250 feet, 8 inches, and is bordered by steel netting for deck personnel safety. The deck itself is made of high-strength steel coated with MS-375G Kevlar ablative, which gives it a nonslip surface and provides protection for the deck. The flight deck has an angled deck, set at 14 degrees off-center, which has a dual function: it acts as the landing area for recovering aircraft, and it provides room for aircraft to be launched simultaneously from the bow catapults.

The flight deck has four type C Mk. 13 Mod 1 catapults, which are 310 feet long and operate at 1,000 psi (6.9 MPa). These catapult can launch one aircraft per minute and are capable of accelerating an aircraft from 0 to 160 knots in less than three seconds. Just behind each of them, there is a jet blast deflector, which is elevated to a 45-degree angle during launch to deflect jet exhaust away from the deck. These deflectors are made of concrete and contain an embedded seawater cooling system to avoid damage from the hot engine exhaust. Each of the deflectors has six sections that can be independently moved.

Some aircraft parked on the USS *Nimitz* flight deck during heavy rain.
US Navy photo / MC3 Raul Moreno Jr.

Impressive nocturnal shot of the flight operations onboard the USS *Nimitz. US Navy photo / MC3 Raul Moreno Jr.*

An exhaust deflector is raised prior to a launching. *US Navy photo / MC3 Raul Moreno Jr.*

An E-2D Hawkeye prepares to be launched from the USS *Nimitz* flight deck.
US Navy photo / MC3 Raul Moreno Jr.

An F/A-18D Hornet and an E/A-6B Prowler are being positioned and secured on elevator 3 in order to be brought to the flight deck aboard the nuclear-powered aircraft carrier USS *Nimitz* (CVN-68) in the Pacific Ocean on March 24, 2009. *US Marine Corps photo by Lance Cpl. Matthew Lemieux / Released*

A pair of "Legacy Hornets" parked on one of the elevators of the USS *Nimitz. US Navy photo / MC3 Chris Bartlett*

A VMFA-323 and an F/A-18C Hornet fighter on one of the elevators of the USS *Nimitz*. US Navy photo / MC3 Chris Bartlett

Red Sea, 2013. Sailors take part in a small-arms-fire practice on elevator 3 by the hangar bay of the aircraft carrier USS *Nimitz. US Navy photo by Mass Communication Specialist Seaman Eric M. Butler*

To transport aircraft from the hangar to the flight deck, there are four elevators: three on the starboard side (two forward and one aft of the island superstructure) and one on the port side. Each elevator, which is made of aluminum, measures 52 feet wide by 70 feet long inboard and 85 feet long outboard. The total area of each elevator measures 3,880 square feet. Each is capable of supporting 47 tons.

The aircraft are recovered by using the Mk. 7 Mod 3 arresting gear system, which consists of four arresting cables and an emergency crash barrier at the rear of the carrier's flight deck. The arresting cables are made of 7/16-inch-thick, braided, polyester-core, flattened-strand steel and are numbered 1 through 4 from back to front. Each of them is spaced approximately 50 feet apart and stretches across the entire angled flight deck.

The so-called island is the central command-and-control facility for the carrier and for air operations. It comprises the bridge, flag bridge, and primary flight control center, also known as Pri-Fly. It is located on the top or 010 level of the island; just aft is the open area called "Vulture's Row," where crew can observe air operations without the hazards inherent on the flight deck. Just below Pri-Fly is the bridge, from which the carrier's commanding and executive officers control and navigate the carrier.

Flag plot is located below the bridge on the 08 level and is where the commanding admiral or Combat Strike Group commander can observe operations.

Nimitz has had the top two levels of its island altered and a new integrated mast/antenna shelter installed.

Western Pacific Ocean, 2005. An F/A-18 Hornet of VFA-137 "Kestrels" squadron catches the arresting-gear four-guide wire aboard the flight deck of the USS *Nimitz*. *US Navy photo by Photographer's Mate Airman Justin R. Blake*

Midshipman 1st Class Joseph Martin, *right*, from the University of Oklahoma, observes flight operations with Aviation Boatswain's Mate (Handling) 2nd Class Jared Whitefield from primary flight control aboard the aircraft carrier USS *Nimitz* as part of Operation Enduring Freedom. *US Navy photo by MCS3 Raul Moreno Jr.*

Close-up shot of a navigational device. *US Navy photo / MCSN Kole E. Carpenter*

An aircraft handler aboard the USS *Nimitz* makes his duty using the radio. *US Navy photo / MC3 (SW) Nathan R. McDonald*

Specialist sailors take care of the USS *Nimitz* guidance. *US Navy photo / MC3 Raul Moreno Jr.*

Sailors perform navigational calculations on the bridge of the USS *Nimitz. US Navy photo / MCSN Kole E. Carpenter*

Indian Ocean, June 11, 2013. Operations Specialist Seaman Domonique Smith marks contacts on the ships radar on the bridge of the USS *Nimitz*. The *Nimitz* Strike Group was deployed to the US 5th Fleet area of responsibility conducting maritime security operations and theater security cooperation efforts. *US Navy photo by Mass Communication Specialist 3rd Class Derek W. Volland*

A sailor using the radio aboard the USS *Nimitz. US Navy photo / MC3 Raul Moreno Jr.*

Specialists navigate the USS *Nimitz*. US Navy photo / MCSN Kole E. Carpenter

A specialist takes care of the aircraft status on the *Nimitz* flight deck. *US Navy photo / MC3 (SW) Nathan R. McDonald*

Specialists monitor flight
operations aboard the USS *Nimitz.*
*US Navy photo / MCSN
Kole E. Carpenter*

As for internal sections, they are divided into various levels, all referenced from the hangar deck (located just below the flight deck), which can store fifty aircraft and runs approximately two-thirds of the length of the carrier. Overall, the hangar measures 684 feet long and 108 feet wide and stands 25 feet high. The hangar-area bay is divided into three equal-sized areas and is separated by a series of heavy, armored, antiblast, fireproof doors.

Levels above the hangar are numbered (such as 01 Deck, 02 Deck, and so on), while levels below are known as Second Deck, Third Deck, etc. Most of the air wing and aviation-related command facilities are on 03 Deck, located immediately below the flight deck. On this deck are the following sections: the squadron thick, ready rooms (one per squadron), air wing offices and command spaces, berthing, and the wardroom.

Forward of the ready rooms is an area with limited personnel traffic that houses the flag staff, central command, and control suites. It comprises the Combat Information/Direction Center (the overall combat command facility, overseeing all information whether obtained from ship sensors, aircraft, or external intelligence sources), which has several subcompartments dedicated to antisurface warfare, antiair warfare, undersea warfare, and electronic warfare. These sections are physically separated, which limits the effects of battle damage on command functions. From that center, the overall battle can be conducted; other sections include the Tactical Flag Command Center, Ships Signals Exploitation Space; Carrier Air Traffic Control Center (which manages all air operations and air traffic control around the Combat Strike Group, being responsible for communicating with all aircraft outside the 5-mile radius; within that radius, control is handed to the air boss in Pri-Fly, and subsequently to the landing signal officer); Ships Signals Exploitation Space (whose function is to process and exploit electronic signals of interest; its members have access to the highest level of intelligence); Tactical Flag Command Center, which a scaled-down version of the Combat Information Center, from where high ranked officers and the Combat Strike Group commander can conduct Combat Strike Group operations by means of USQ-81(V) 20-square-foot large-screen displays for viewing information.

Gulf of Oman, June 29, 2012. Sailors perform maintenance on an F/A-18C Hornet assigned to the VFA-146 "Blue Diamonds" squadron aboard the USS *Nimitz* during Operation Enduring Freedom. *US Navy photo by Mass Communication Specialist 3rd Class Phil Ladouceur*

Arabian Gulf, July 10, 2013. Sailors install a motor rotor blade on an MH-60S Seahawk helicopter assigned to the "Indians" of Helicopter Sea Combat Squadron (HSC) 6 in the hangar bay on board the USS *Nimitz*. The *Nimitz* Strike Group was deployed to the US 5th Fleet area of responsibility conducting maritime security operations, theater security cooperation efforts and support missions for Operation Enduring Freedom. *US Navy Photo by Mass Communication Specialist 3rd Class Chris Bartlett*

Gulf of Oman, August 5, 2013. Aviation Electronics Technician 2nd Class Alyssa Poole works on an MH-60S Seahawk assigned to the HSC-6 "Indians" squadron in the hangar bay of the aircraft carrier USS *Nimitz* during Operation Enduring Freedom. *US Navy photo by Mass Communication Specialist 3rd Class Chris Bartlett*

Gulf of Oman, July 1, 2013. A midshipman practices a fast-roping technique as part of a tour of an explosive-ordnance disposal unit onboard the aircraft carrier USS *Nimitz* during Operation Enduring Freedom. *US Navy photo by Mass Communication Specialist Seaman Apprentice Victoria I. Ochoa*

Gulf of Oman, July 1, 2013. Explosive Ordnance Disposal 1st Class Thomas Hensen gives midshipmen basic training on explosive-ordnance disposal techniques onboard the aircraft carrier USS *Nimitz*, then deployed to support missions for Operation Enduring Freedom. *US Navy photo / Mass Communication Specialist Seaman Apprentice Victoria I. Ochoa*

Sailors perform physical exercises in the *Nimitz* hangar bay. *US Navy photo / MC2 Devin Wray*

North Arabian Sea, January, 1, 2010. Sailors stand watch in the Combat Direction Center aboard the USS *Nimitz* (CVN-68) at midnight, New Year's Eve, during a *Nimitz* Carrier Strike Group routine deployment to the region. *US Navy photo by Mass Communications Specialist 1st David Mercil*

Gulf of Oman, June 16, 2013. Sailors compete in a biathlon in the hangar bay of the aircraft carrier USS *Nimitz*, during the ship's deployment to support Operation Enduring Freedom. *US Navy photo by Mass Communication Specialist Seaman Derek A. Harkins*

The *Nimitz* has ten firewall bulkheads, twenty-three watertight transverse bulkheads, and more than 2,000 compartments, which house all the installations needed to provide the best conditions to its crew, including gym rooms, a complete hospital equipped for any surgical treatment, and meal/living rooms.

Gulf of Oman, June 16, 2013. Lt. David Schultz, from Ft. Myers, Florida, competes in a biathlon in the hangar bay of the USS *Nimitz*, then deployed to the support missions for Operation Enduring Freedom. *US Navy photo by Mass Communication Specialist Seaman Derek A. Harkins*

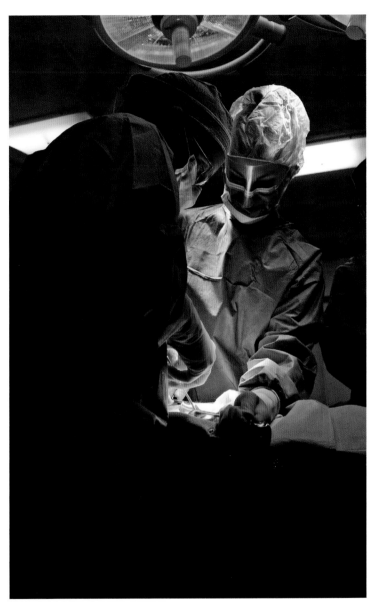

A medical team performs a surgical procedure aboard the USS *Nimitz*. *US Navy photo / MCSA Kelly M. Agee*

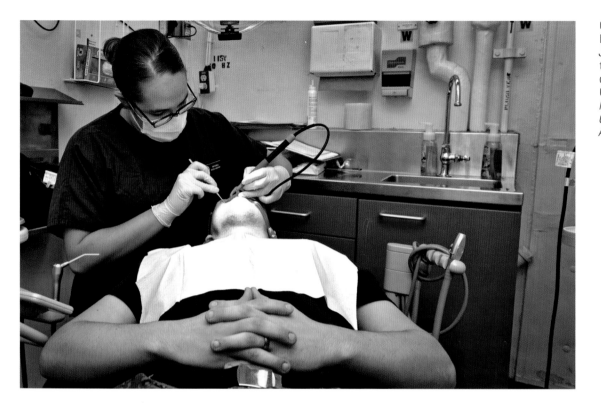

Gulf of Oman, August 3, 2013. Hospital Corpsman 3rd Class Jessica Bureau cleans a patient's teeth aboard the USS *Nimitz*, then deployed to support missions for Operation Enduring Freedom. *US Navy photo by Mass Communication Specialist Seaman Apprentice Aiyana Paschal*

Arabian Sea, August 31, 2013. Food service personnel serve chow in the aft mess decks aboard the USS *Nimitz*, then deployed to the US 5th Fleet area of responsibility, conducting maritime security operations. *US Navy photo by Mass Communication Specialist Seaman Kole E. Carpenter*

Preparing hamburgers onboard the USS *Nimitz* kitchen. *US Navy photo / MCSA Kelly M. Agee*

Indian Ocean, June 9, 2013. Culinary Specialist 3rd Class Kenra Bellinger prepares a freshly cooked meal to be served during a Sunday brunch on the mess decks of the USS *Nimitz*. *US Navy photo by Mass Communication Specialist Seaman Derek A. Harkins*

Sailors in one of the USS *Nimitz's* meal areas. *US Navy photo / MC3 Linda S. Swearingen*

Gulf of Oman, June 24, 2013. A group of midshipmen eat lunch with Capt. Jeff Ruth, commanding officer of the aircraft carrier USS *Nimitz* (then deployed to support missions for Operation Enduring Freedom). *US Navy photo by Mass Communication Specialist 3rd Class Jess Lewis*

The ship's tasks are coordinated by a complete array of electronics systems dedicated to command and control, electronic warfare, and navigation / target search / weapons guidance roles.

As for command and control, there are the OE-82, AN/SSR-1, WSC-3, and Naval Tactical Datalink Systems. Looking at every of these systems in some detail, the first three of them are part of the *Nimitz*'s Satellite Communication system: the OE-82 is the system's antenna, the AN/SSR-1 is its receiver (consisting of up to four AS-2815/SSR-1 antennas with an amplifier-converter, AM-6534/SSR-1, for each antenna), and the WSC-3 is the system's transceiver, designed primarily for shipboard installation. The antenna is attached to a pedestal that permits it to rotate so that the antenna is always in view of the satellite. The frequency band for receiving is 248 to 272 MHz, while the band for transmitting is 292 to 312 MHz, and the antennas are used to receive satellite fleet broadcasts at frequencies of 240 to 315 MHz. The antenna and converters are mounted above deck so that at least one of them is always in view of the satellite.

The Naval Tactical Datalink System is one of the most important systems aboard the USS *Nimitz*. It is the first part of a two-part system, the other being the Airborne Tactical Datalink System. The former is installed aboard ships, while the latter is installed in aircraft; they operate together in order to provide an exchange of information between a vessel and airplanes. The Naval Tactical Datalink System is made up of standard peripherals, displays, computers, and datalinks, as well as manual-entry devices, antisubmarine warfare systems, missile systems, gun systems, electronic countermeasures systems, and ship attitude sensors. In order to make possible for the Naval Tactical Data System to accomplish its objectives in real time, the system receives data from various sensing devices that are in continuous contact with the outside environment. It uses these data to evaluate an event as it happens. How often the system requires an update will determine the rate of sampling for each sensing device. The design philosophy of the Naval Tactical Datalink System is per the "unit computer concept" (i.e., a set of standard computers operating in conjunction with each other to increase capacity and functional capability). The Naval Tactical Datalink System integrates all systems and subsystems for performing the basic combat system functions, such as detection and entry, tracking and identification, threat evaluation and weapon assignment, and, finally, engagement and engagement assessment. The Naval Tactical Datalink System accomplishes its tasks by receiving, storing, and processing the data inputs from the other systems and subsystems. The operational program then distributes the processed data as usable inputs for other systems and subsystems. The data display also allows the operator to interact with the system.

The Naval Tactical Datalink System's other part, the Airborne Tactical Datalink System, receives instructions from the former (such as target quantity, direction, speed, and altitude) and acts according to these instructions in order to neutralize the threat in the best possible way. It is installed into aircraft such as the Boeing F/A-18E/F Super Hornet, the US Navy's current standard aircraft for offensive and defensive missions.

As for electronic warfare, the USS *Nimitz* is equipped with two SLQ-32(V)4 systems, eight Mk. 36 SRBOC Decoy launchers, one SLQ-49 Floating decoy system, one SLQ-39 Chaff buoy system, one SSQ-95 Floating jammer system, and two SLQ-25 Nixie Torpedo decoy systems.

The SLQ-32(V) 4 system is a modular electronic-warfare suite that uses the multibeam system concept to form electronically scannable fan beams that can rapidly detect and locate signals and concentrate jamming power on sources identified as hostile. The system generates signals to decoy hostile systems into a false determination of the carrying ship's location. It protects the ship by initiating the use of chaff or decoys (or both) along with the jamming signals, by means of an UYK-19(V) computer and a Super Rapid Bloom Off-Board chaff launcher. This variant was developed for installation on aircraft carriers. The basic system is the same as the (V)3 variant, with fiber-optic interfaces added to accommodate the large physical distance between units. The (V)3 has two more racks of EW hardware to provide an active electronic countermeasures capability. The racks include eight high-voltage power supplies for the traveling wave tubes (TWTs), a digital switching unit, a transponder, and a techniques generator. The computer's memory capacity was increased from 64K to 80K.

To accommodate Band-3 transmitter antennas (one pair in each assembly), the outboard antenna assemblies are expanded and given hydraulic roll stabilization. The SLQ-32(V)3 detects and identifies emitter transmissions in the 250 MHz to 20 GHz range and jams hostile Band-3 emitters. Beam-forming lens arrays and semi-omni-directional antennas drive crystal video receivers and instantaneous frequency measurement receivers, respectively. Angle and amplitude samples are sent in digital format to the Direction/Frequency Correlator. Frequency samples are also sent to this device, where they are compared to, and matched with, known threat samples. A digital tracking unit compares each new pulse with a frequency/angle matrix corresponding to the current emitter activity being tracked. That unit updates the UYK-19(V) central processor with changes in the radar environment, such as changes in emitter angle (movement), the appearance of a new emitter (new signal), or the disappearance of a previous emitter (turnoff, cessation, or neutralization of previous threat).

The Mk. 36 Super Rapid Blooming Off-Board Countermeasures being deployed. *US Navy-MC3 William Dodge*

The SLQ-32(V) 4 can jam multiple Band-3 threats simultaneously by using repeater or transponder techniques, or both. A Command Generator Unit produces the required countermeasures waveforms and modulation.

The Mk. 36 Super Rapid Blooming Off-Board Countermeasures (SRBOC) decoy launchers are expendable countermeasure launchers. The system includes control and power systems, with both launcher and load configurations tailored to provide the maximum protection for a specific vessel type.

The deck-mounted launcher features six launch tubes, arranged in pairs set at elevation angles of 45º and 60º, respectively. Electromagnetic-induction firing circuits set off a squib in the expendable cartridge, igniting a charge that propels the chaff cartridge or flares into the air.

A master launcher control provides both manual firing circuits and status indicators and is typically located in the Combat Control Center. A bridge launcher control provides auxiliary firing circuits and status indicators for the bridge. The power supply system provides the firing power for the firing circuits and includes a standby battery and trickle charger for backup and emergency operation. Ready service lockers store up to thirty-five expendable cartridges adjacent to the launchers.

The chaff deployed by SRBOC forms a cloud at just under 1,000 feet of altitude, which confuses or degrades fire control radars and active missile seeker heads. This way, the attacking radar seeker tends to identify a point in the chaff cloud rather than the ship as the target center, drawing the warhead away from the vessel. Larger ships need more than the two cartridges, launched in salvo fashion to create a sufficiently large and properly shaped decoy to protect the ship.

The infrared countermeasures are flares that, when launched, float under a parachute. The high-intensity infrared source presents the missile's seeker head with a larger heat source than the ship, decoying heat-seeking missiles away from the ship. Most detonate on the basis of the decoying signal rather than impact, and the vessel is therefore protected from the weapon.

The system's barrel diameter is 5.1 inches and is composed by launcher, power supply, launcher control (bridge), launcher control (master), and ready service lockers (thirty-five rounds). The system can deploy chaff as far as 1.32 nautical miles from the ship.

The SLQ-49 floating decoy system, also known as Rubber Duck, is an expendable missile decoy system tasked with seducing radar-homing air-to-surface missiles by providing full radar cross-section decoy targets. It provides protection of surface ships from sustained missile attack, by supplying a long-endurance floating decoy with ship-like radar cross sections. The system is composed of a broadband, response-passive, octahedral, radar decoy reflector mounted in life-raft-type containers. Launched from a simple unit and operating in linked pairs, these reflectors provide a good horizontal and azimuth response to counter threat emitters. A standard installation includes two rail launchers and eight linked pairs of decoys per ship. Irvin has also developed a remote facility permitting the Replica system to be pre-positioned and activated on command.

Its deployment is effected by suspending the system from the leeward side of the vessel and inflating the unit by means of the ship's compressed-air or bottled-gas supply. When inflated, Rubber Duck comprises a substantial structure that remains operational for up to three hours in Sea State 4 conditions. A lid of the launch container remains attached to each unit, acting as a drag anchor. It limits the decoy's drift speed to no more than one-quarter of the prevailing wind speed and prevents the two reflectors from collapsing together. The two decoys are linked to each other by means of a cord. The system's features are as follows: container diameter, 22 inches; container weight, 147.5 pounds; launcher height, 56 inches; launcher width, 52 inches; and launcher weight, 381 pounds.

The SLQ-25 Nixie Torpedo decoy is a torpedo countermeasures set (i.e., a noisemaker) for surface warships, being a towed electro-acoustic device designed to provide surface ships with countermeasures against homing torpedoes. When combined with command/display and information-processing systems, the SLQ-25(V) becomes a major component of the Ship Acoustic and Torpedo Countermeasures system. It features a modular design that is digitally controlled, with a digital interface to other shipboard systems. The system can use either copper or fiber-optic connections shipboard, with a fiber-optic connection to the towed decoy. Nixie detects and classifies torpedo threats and attempts to counter the acoustic sensor or the seeker head of the torpedo by generating decoy signals that are tailored to attract the attacking torpedo, luring it away from the ship. A complex set of signal emulators can be programmed to emulate the desired acoustic signature.

It is made up of two towed devices, below-decks electronics cabinets, and control consoles. A typical installation entails two winches deploying two Nixie acoustic projectors via a cable deployed over the ship's transom. A fiber-optic strand is included in the tow cable to interface with the SLQ-25A Towed Array Sensor. It is controlled via the cable with a modular, digital-control system. A single-winch version is available for ships with limited space or weight restrictions. The towed device receives the torpedo's "ping" frequency, amplifies it two or three times, and sends it back to lure the torpedo away. It detects incoming torpedoes and provides data to the Multi-Sensor Torpedo Recognition and Alertment Processor. This unit performs the necessary signal processing and controls the decoys in order to detect, classify, and localize torpedoes. It also provides command and control information, target motion analysis, threat evaluation, and tactical advice to the ship's crew. It has displays with automatic visual and audio alarms to alert the crew to a threat in the SSQ-95 floating jammer system, which determines the time to deploy countermeasures and perform evasive maneuvers. The system combines inputs from hull-mounted sonars, towed arrays, sonobuoys, and the SLQ-25B.

The system features an open architecture, which will facilitate future enhancements, including hardware or software upgrades. A Launched Expendable Acoustic Decoy can be rocket- or mortar-launched from a standard Mk. 36 SRBOC launcher. The decoy performs the same function as the towed countermeasure.

A Tripwire Torpedo Defense System has been developed, which provides additional sensors for the SLQ-25A and an Anti-Torpedo All-Up-Round countermeasure.

Operationally, the towed bodies are streamed out behind the ship or launched from a standard decoy launcher. They act to detect and locate torpedoes and other acoustic targets. One towed countermeasure is operated while the other is on standby in case the first is hit by a torpedo and put out of operation. The emitted signal is intended to decoy the torpedo away from the ship, where it will explode harmlessly. Nixie simulates a variety of propeller and machinery noises at frequencies and modulations tailored to attract and counter specific torpedo threats. The outputs are designed to match the particular acoustic signatures of the target or create enough nonspecific acoustic noise to confuse the seeker. The system provides coverage astern, normally a blind area.

The SLQ-25(V) detects and identifies acoustic sensors such as sonar- and acoustic-homing torpedoes. It creates noise signals to jam the sensors, incapacitating the sonar or deflecting the homing torpedo, and alerts the system operator so the ship can take defensive and evasive actions, if needed.

The system is made up of the SLQ-25A Towed Acoustic Countermeasure, Multi-Sensor Torpedo Recognition and Alertment Processor, and Launched Expendable Acoustic Decoy.

Its physical features are 66 × 25 × 22 inches and 852 pounds (dimensions and weight form the Towed Acoustic Countermeasure); 72 × 25 × 22 inches and 660 pounds (dimensions and weight for the SLQ-25A Multi-Sensor Torpedo Recognition and Alertment Processor, respectively); 6 × 47 inches and 58 pounds (the TB-14A Towered Pod); and 5.125 × 48.5 inches and 55 pounds (for the Mk. 12 Launched Expendable Acoustic Decoy).

Finally, the SLQ-39 chaff buoy system is released from the LAU-126 sonobuoy launcher, which contains a single buoy. The chaff itself is 36.08 inches, with a 4.93-inch diameter, and weighs 38 pounds.

Regarding the remaining tasks, the USS *Nimitz* is equipped with one SPS-48E 3-D air search radar, one SPS-49(V)5 2-D air search radar, one SPS-67(V)1 surface search radar, one Mk. 23 target acquisition radar, six Mk. 95 missile fire control radars, one SPS-64 (V)9, one Furuno 900 navigation color radar, and, finally, one SPN-44 radar.

The SPS-48E is a long-range, 3-D shipboard, air surveillance radar. SPS-48 upgrade efforts resulted in the development of the SPS-48E for the Navy's New Threat Upgrade program. This radar includes major improvements in video processing, jamming countermeasures, and tracking capability. It also modified the antenna, receiver, and control units and replaced the transmitter, data processor, and control consoles.

The SPS-48E was designed to improve the early detection of antiship missiles. Adaptive Doppler processing provides for rapid response to low- and high-flying targets, with low false-alarm rates. The radar can supply positional information for midcourse guidance of the Extended-Range Terrier/Tartar and SM-2 missile systems. The result is essentially a new radar, and SPS-48(V)s already on ships are replaced entirely.

The SPS-48E is installed on aircraft carriers and other new-build ships. It features four scan modes, and only four controls are needed to operate the radar. The system gives higher elevation angle coverage, increased azimuth coverage, increased average power output, better reliability resulting from the use of solid-state components, and frequency and pattern flexibility to allow the defeat of electronic countermeasures jamming while also detecting targets in conditions of heavy clutter.

The SPS-48E antenna was designed to function in very inclement conditions, including wind speeds of up to 75 knots, shock, vibration, ice loading of up to 22 kg/m^2, salt encrustation, and temperature extremes ranging from 48° to +85° C. The NTU system has reduced the overall number of electronic components, simplified maintenance adjustments, and enhanced the built-in test capability of the hardware. The Ultra-Low Side-Lobe Antenna makes target detection possible in the presence of jamming.

The upgrades involve a number of components that vary by platform and can be divided into the following segments: the new Standard SM-2 Block II missile, fire control engagement system modifications, and significant improvement to the SPS-48 and SPS-49 air search radars.

The main application for the SPS-48E is surface ship antiair warfare, and the upgrades enhance the ability to counter the latest

An electronic warfare technician (EN) examines the SLQ-25 (Nixie) torpedo countermeasures equipment of the same model as installed on the USS *Nimitz*. *US Navy*

hostile missile threats. The SPS-48E features greatly reduced antenna side lobes, doubled average transmitter power, adaptive energy beam management, snap-off/snap-on operation, a computer-driven control/display system, a solid-state transmitter, digital subsystem upgrades, improved signal processing, and improved tracking performance. The SPS-48E can automatically track hundreds of aircraft over a vast area.

The pulse Doppler upgrade will make it possible to track small radar cross-section targets such as cruise missiles over land and sea and in ducted clutter. This makes it possible to use the radar to control the skies both over the open ocean and shoreline. The SPS-48E will thus be suitable for littoral operations. The SPS-48E was designed as a direct replacement for the SPS-48C. The antenna weighs 1,700 pounds more because of enhancements that improve side-lobe suppression. Vertical coverage is increased and improved. Adaptive energy beam management and a three-mode, solid-state transmitter improve performance. Ongoing modification work has included the use of fiber-optic cables for SPS-48Es going on aircraft carriers.

The radar's antenna has ninety-five elements, weighs 6,600 pounds, and measures 17.9×16.9 feet, while its operational parameters are as follows: power is 2.2 MW peak, with a 33 kW average; frequency is 2.9 to 3.1 GHz; pulse width is 9 and 27 μsec; pulse repetition frequency is 330 to 2,250 pulses per second; ranges are 230 nm against an aircraft coming at a low angle, 220 nautical miles against a $5m^2$ target, 125 nautical miles against a $1m^2$ target, and 17 nautical miles against a $0.1m^2$ target; elevation coverage is 0° to 45° (search) and 0° to 69° (track); scan rate is fifteen rotations per minute; altitude limit is 100,000 feet; and mean time between failures is higher than 650 hours.

The SPS-49(V)5 2-D is a shipborne air search radar. Its antenna is mechanically stabilized relative to the horizon, making low-altitude detection possible in most sea states. True or relative antenna azimuth information is provided to the ship's radar switchboard in one-speed synchro format, together with time-aligned video and trigger information. This can be distributed throughout the ship. The system includes automatic target detection using pulse Doppler techniques, and clutter maps to enhance target detection in a clutter environment. It has an advanced electronic counter-countermeasures capability as well as an up-to-date, adaptive Digital Moving-Target Indicator and Constant False-Alarm Rate receivers for reliable detection in clutter conditions. It is compatible with standard shipboard displays. Line-of-sight stabilization keeps the antenna beam aligned with the horizon. A characteristic fan-shaped feed horn is underslung in front of an open-mesh, orange-peel parabolic antenna. The fully coherent,

solid-state driver and klystron amplifier chain provide the peak power. Stability is emphasized for improved pulse Doppler processing. It can be pulse repetition frequency staggered and is frequency agile.

A triple-conversion receiver provides image rejection and freedom from spurious responses. Two complete channels are provided for the main and side-lobe blanking channels. The radar features built-in redundancy switches so the side-lobe channel can be substituted for the main channel in case of failure.

Dispersive delay lines are used in both channels to generate and receive the chirp pulse compression signal. A new stable-frequency synthesizer is used for frequency stability and allows instantaneous random frequency selection. There is a four-loop, coherent side-lobe canceler system. The signal processor receives main and side-lobe channel inputs, digitizing them and feeding into side-lobe blanking and interference cancelers. The main channel is processed to provide clutter suppression in a five Flight Information Region filter pulse Doppler processor with false-alarm control. This is followed by the provision of high-resolution clutter maps, video integration, and detection thresholding. The output is usually made up of digital target reports. There is also automatic online fault monitoring and fault isolation. The Radar Set Control allows for manual selection of the radar operating mode, scan rate, emission controls, electronic counter-countermeasures, and fault monitoring. Normal operation is from a set in the Combat Information Center and in the radar room as well.

SPS-49(V) 5 narrow-beam and line-of-sight horizon-stabilized capabilities provide excellent low-altitude target acquisition in all sea states and have enhanced electronic counter-countermeasures processing and automatic target detection capability. Its quality and reliability were upgraded under the Navy Radar Surveillance Equipment program. Plans included development of a medium-pulse repetition frequency upgrade, the addition of the SYS-2(V) to integrate the outputs of the radar to a ship's overall weapons control system, engagement system modifications, and the resolution of production and technical problems. Improvements have also concentrated on efforts to improve the way that ships use the data from all its sensors, fusing more-effective own-ship and cooperative-engagement-capability information into a comprehensive situational awareness for all ships in a battle group. The system's technical data are as follows: antenna weight, 3,165 pounds; below-deck weight, 14,004 pounds; antenna dimensions, 24×14.2 feet; power, 360 kW peak and 13 kW average; frequency, 850 to 942 MHz (fixed or agile); pulse width, 125 μsec or 2 μsec; ranges, from 0.5 nautical mile to 250 nautical miles; scan rate, 6 or 12 rotations per minute; and mean time between failures, higher than 600 hours.

An SPS-48B search radar on the USS *Theodore Roosevelt*. The SPN PL-173P carrier-controlled approach (CCA) radar is seen at the upper left, while the SPS-65 antennas of the Mk. 91 Fire Control System are at the bottom left. The small white bar antenna is the SPS-64(V)9 radar unit. *US Navy*

Arabian Gulf, March 4, 2016. Electronics Technician 3rd Class Jordan Issler conducts maintenance on a radar aboard aircraft carrier USS *Harry S. Truman*. The *Harry S. Truman* Carrier Strike Group was then deployed in support of Operation Inherent Resolve. *US Navy photo by Mass Communication Specialist 3rd Class Justin R. Pacheco*

The AN/SPS-67 radar is a short-range, two-dimensional, surface-search/navigation pulsed radar system that provides highly accurate surface and limited low-flyer detection and tracking capabilities. It provides excellent performance in rain and sea clutter and is useful in harbor navigation, since it is also capable of detecting buoys and small obstructions without difficulty. The construction of the radar set is primarily solid state.

It operates in the 5450 to 5825 MHz range, using a coaxial magnetron as the transmitter output tube. The transmitter/receiver is capable of operation in a long (1.0 second), medium (0.25 millisecond), or short (0.10 millisecond) pulse mode to enhance radar performance for specific operational or tactical situations. Pulse repetition frequencies (PRFs) of 750, 1,200, and 2,400 pulses per second are used for the long, medium, and short pulse modes, respectively.

Some special operating features included in the AN/SPS-67(V) radars are as follows: automatic frequency control, automatic tuning, fast time constant, interference suppression, anti-log circuit (target enhance), sensitivity time control, video clutter suppression, built-in test equipment, sector radiate, ship's heading marker, jitter mode, and stagger mode. The equipment's basic technical data are as follows: maximum range, 56.2 nautical miles; rotations per minute, 15/30; azimuth, 1.5°; elevation, 12°; and power, 280 kW.

The Mk 23 Target Acquisition System is a sea-based, two-dimensional, D-band device and operates as a range-gated, pulse Doppler radar system. Its "identification friend or foe" antenna is mounted back to back with the search antenna. Transmitted energy is concentrated in the lower elevations of a fan-shaped beam, designed to be especially sensitive to low-level, sea-skimming targets. The feed system uses upward of twenty-six flared feed horns and has a side-lobe blanking system. It is part of the Improved Point Defense Missile System, which is a surface-to-air system that provides a ship with defense from an antiship missile threat. It reacts automatically to threats in a variety of environmental and weather conditions, being formed through the integration of the RIM-7 NATO Sea Sparrow point defense missile system, fire control unit, launch system, and the Mk. 23 Target Acquisition System. Although developed as a subsystem to that system, the Mk. 23 can designate targets for other weapon systems, such as guns. It can detect targets in clutter and discriminate between targets in an electronic-countermeasures environment. The UYA-4 console contains the controls and indicators for launch system assignment, missile frequency assignment, missile run-up, firing orders, and status monitoring. It also allows the firing officer to override the automatic operation at any time during the target engagement sequence.

The Mk. 23 Target Acquisition System can track friendly ships in the area as well, allowing for safer gun operations. The system has four operating modes: normal point defense mode, which is used to detect, identify, and track missiles at a range beyond 20 nautical miles and engages them with antimissile missiles; surveillance or medium-range mode, which offers a 90-plus-nautical-mile detection range for surveillance and air traffic control; and, finally, the mixed mode, which is a combination of normal point defense and long-range modes. Emission control permits the operator to scan selected corridors and switches the system on and off to avoid detection by hostile radio finder collection systems. The Model 1 provides direct computer-to-computer interface with the NATO Sea Sparrow missile and with a ship's tactical data system. The Mk. 23 Target Acquisition System's operational characteristics are as follows: antenna weight, 2,000 pounds; antenna height, 129 inches; antenna width, 231 inches; depth, 76 inches; frequency, 1–2 GHz; scan rate, 15 or 30 rotations per minute; elevation coverage, 0-75°; azimuth coverage, 360°; vertical coverage, 90°; power, 200 kW (peak); ranges, from 20 nm (1m^2 target) to 100 nautical miles (secondary surveillance); and target capacity, fifty-four simultaneous targets.

The Mk. 95 is continuous-wave fire control radar associated with the short-range NATO Sea Sparrow Missile System. Side-by-side Mk. 95 parabolic transmitting and Cassegrain lenses receiving I-band antennas ride on a single pedestal mounted near the eight-cell launcher. The transmitter's radome is convex; the receiver's is concave. In order to expand the tracker's field of view, the Mk. 95 uses a wide-beam illuminator that allows the missile to use proportional navigation. An electro-optical tracker fitted between the Mk. 95s provides an alternate tracking method in conditions of high electronic counter-countermeasures.

The SPS-64(V) is the primary navigation radar, with an electronic-support-measures interface, which prevents interference from other ship radars. A fire control interface distributes video, trigger, and azimuth information to the ship's fire control systems. It can provide data to one or more SPA-25 indicators, as well as a blanking signal to the SLA-10 Blanker / Video Mixer Group, and can accept a ship's gyro inputs. The SPS-64(V) is made up of a high-powered S-band search radar, a 12-foot antenna array (AS-3195), a 60 kW S-band receiver-transmitter (RT-1241A), a 50 kW X-band receiver/transmitter (RT-1342B), a RAYCAS V CIC 16-inch Bright Display (target tracking, navigation, and tactical data), and a RAYPATH 12- or 16-inch Bright Display (radar information, collision avoidance, navigation data).

The RT1246A Receiver Transmitter operates at 9.3 MHz, with a peak power output of 20 kW. The antenna array provides a rate of thirty-three rotation per minute, with a 1.2° horizontal bandwidth. Contact data are updated every two seconds. The Interswitch Unit (SA-2308) makes it possible to select any indicator/receiver/transmitter combination.

The X-band system provides better resolution in standard weather conditions and is more suitable for harbor and river navigation. In good weather conditions, the S-band radar provides better range performance on low-lying targets just above sea level.

As a backup, either radar can be connected to either indicator. The S-band radar has been shown to give 30–60 percent better range performance than the X-band system in heavy rain. As a result, S-band radars display small targets in dense sea clutter at two to three times greater range than the X-band.

The Electronic Support Measures Interface provides two blanking pulse outputs, one for each radar transmitter, which can be connected to any Electronic Support Measures system or used to prevent interference with other radars.

A fire control interface conditions and distributes radar video, trigger, and azimuth information to the ship's fire control system. It can use the SPS-64 as a backup or alternate sensor. The interface also allows the fire control radar data to be displayed on the RAYCAS V or RAYPATH indicators. There is a synchronization mode that allows the X-band navigation radar transmitter to be slaved to the fire control radar to prevent interference.

The system is adapted for close-in navigation in harbor channels and congested waterways, as well as longer-range surveillance as needed. The radar provides all-weather performance. Display choices include relative, true motion, and collision avoidance modes. The displays feature direct daylight viewing or effective night operations without a hood.

The true-motion unit electronically plots and shows the true or relative course of up to eight selected targets. The anticollision unit automatically evaluates a target's track to instantaneously determine a collision avoidance course (or target intercept course). The system's technical information is as follows: antenna weight, 332 pounds; antenna size, 6 × 9 × 12 feet; frequencies, 9375 ± 25 MHz and 3030 ± 25 MHz; pulse repetition frequency (pulses per second) 900, 1,800, 3,600, 900, 1,800, 3,600; peak power, 10, 25, 50, and 60 kW; range, from 20 yards to 64 nautical miles; pulse width (μsec), 0.06, 0.5, 1 0.06, 0.5, 1.0; and scan rate, 33 rpm 33 rpm.

Finally, the AN/SPN-44 is a range-rate radar set that computes, indicates, and records the speed of aircraft making a landing approach to the carrier. Both true and relative air speed are indicated. Supplied with this accurate information on the speed of the approaching aircraft, the landing signal officer can wave off those attempting to land at an unsafe speed.

Regarding self-defense weapons, the USS *Nimitz* has an integrated system made up of weapons to be deployed against aerial threats located at medium, close, and very close ranges. The first of those weapons is the Raytheon RIM-7 Sea Sparrow Missile, which is a radar-guided, air-to-air missile with high explosive warhead. These have a cylindrical body with four wings at midbody and four tail fins. It has all-weather, all-altitude operational capability and can attack high-performance aircraft and missiles from any direction.

In addition to the aerial targets, it can also act against antiship missiles as well as surface missile platforms with surface-to-air missiles by means of its surveillance radar capability. The system consists of a Guided Missile Fire Control System Mk. 91 and a Guided Missile Launching System Mk. 29. The former is a computer-operated fire control system that provides automatic acquisition and tracking of a designated target, generates launcher and missile orders, and, in the automatic mode, initiates the firing command when the target becomes able to be engaged. Although most of the system's operations are carried out under automatic or semiautomatic conditions, it permits operator intervention and override at any time. It is a rapid-reaction, lightweight launching system that provides on-mount stowage and launch capability of up to eight missiles and responds to launcher position commands, missile orders, and control commands. The RIM-7 Sparrow III version utilizes the energy reflected from the target and from rear-reference radio finding (transmitted from the director system) for developing missile wing movement orders enabling target intercept.

The system's technical data are as follows:

Weight	2,980 pounds
Dimensions	12 ft. long x 8 in. diameter; wingspan: 25 in.
Warhead	86 pounds. WAU-17/B blast fragmentation; range, from 1,600 yards to more than 30 nautical miles; speed, more than 2,660 miles per hour

The intermediary section of the USS *Nimitz* defense ring is the General Dynamics (now Raytheon) / Diehl BGT Defence RIM-116 Rolling Airframe Missile. Also known as RAM Mk. 31, it is composed of two major subsystems: the Mk. 49 Guided Missile Launching System and the Mk. 44 Guided Missile Round Pack. The former provides for storage and environmental protection of twenty-one missiles. It receives target designation data from the defense system controller, points the missile toward an intercept trajectory, and controls the missile-firing sequence. The RAM Missile (RIM 116B) is delivered in a sealed container. Together these are designated the

Onboard USS *Harry S. Truman* (CVN 75), a NATO Sea Sparrow missile is launched during a live-fire missile exercise. *Official US Navy photo by Photographer's Mate Second Class (Aviation Warfare) Jason P. Taylor*

USS *Theodore Roosevelt* conducts a live-fire exercise with RAM-116. *US Navy photo*

Also onboard the USS *Harry S. Truman*, sailors who were with the Combat Systems Department, CS7 Division, download the Rolling Airframe Missile System (RAM), which holds a total of twenty-one missiles. *Navy photo by Mass Communication Specialist Third Class Ann Marie Lazarek, released by ENS David Lloyd*

Mk. 44 Mod 2 Guided Missile Round Pack. This item has a ten-year storage life, with no testing or maintenance required. There is provision for a digital data interface (MIL-STD-1553B) with the missile while in the Guided Missile Round Pack. This allows updating the missile-operating software with no disassembly required. The supersonic 5-inch Rolling Airframe Missile was originally developed using existing AIM-9 Sidewinder components. The RAM Missile utilizes the Sidewinder fuse (upgraded for RAM), warhead, and solid-propellant rocket motor. Two variable-incidence canards in conjunction with the rolling airframe and a closed-loop autopilot provide high maneuver capability.

The RAM Missile employs a dual-mode capability against radio-finding radiating targets. A passive radio frequency seeker provides midcourse guidance, and the passive infrared seeker provides terminal guidance. The RAM missile utilizes an image-scan infrared seeker to provide an autonomous infrared acquisition and track mode against non-radio-finding radiating threats. The control section steers and stabilizes the missile by providing a closed-loop autopilot with aerodynamic feedback. The control section processes the acceleration guidance command from the guidance section into a steering command, which actuates the variable-incidence canards to steer the missile to target intercept.

An active optical-proximity fuse initiates warhead detonation. A contact fuse located in the control section provides an alternate method of fusing by detonating the warhead upon target impact.

The Mk. 20 Mod 2 is a narrow-beam, active optical-proximity fuse system that has been adapted from the AIM-9 Sidewinder program to improve performance against antiship cruise missiles at extremely low altitudes over water. The warhead is an annular blast fragmentation device, which uses a conventional high explosive.

The RAM Mk. 1 Mod 0 propulsion section consists of a Mk. 112 Mod 1 reduced-smoke rocket motor, which is also derived from AIM-9 Sidewinder. A folding tail assembly is attached to the rocket motor near the aft end of the motor tube. The four tails are folded when the missile is installed in the canister, and are automatically erect at launch when the missile leaves the canister. The tails are canted slightly from the missile longitudinal axis to sustain missile roll during flight. The inner surface of the canister has four raised spiral rails, which bear against the forward surfaces of the missile tail assembly to develop the initial missile roll during launch.

Technical specifications are as follows:

Weight	launcher, 12,736 pounds; missile, 162 lbs. 1 oz.
Dimensions	missile, 9 ft. 2 in. long; missile wingspan, 17.1 in.
Warhead	blast fragmentation warhead, 24 lbs. 15 oz.; operational range, 5.6 miles; speed, more than Mach 2 (1,522 miles per hour). Guidance system has three modes: passive radio frequency / infrared homing; infrared only; infrared dual mode enabled (radio frequency and infrared homing). Launch platform: Mk. 144 Guided Missile Launcher of the Mk. 49 Guided Missile Launching System

Finally, the inner portion of defense is represented by Mk. 15 Phalanx Close-In Weapon System, which provides ships with a point defense capability against antiship missiles, aircraft, and littoral warfare threats that have penetrated other fleet defenses. It automatically detects, evaluates, tracks, engages, and performs kill assessment against missiles and high-speed aircraft threats. The current Phalanx variant (Block 1B) adds the ability to counter asymmetric warfare threats through the addition of an integrated, stabilized, electro-optic sensor. These improvements give Phalanx the added ability to counter small, high-speed surface craft, aircraft, helicopters, and unmanned aerial systems (UASs). The basic (original) style is the Block 0, equipped with first-generation solid-state electronics and with marginal capability against surface targets. The Block 1 (1988) upgrade offered various improvements in radar, ammunition, rate of fire, engagement elevation (increased to +70 degrees), and computing. These improvements were intended to increase the system's capability against emerging Russian supersonic antiship missiles. Block 1A introduced a new computer system to counter more-maneuverable targets. The Block 1B PSuM (Phalanx Surface Mode, 1999) adds a forward-looking infrared (FLIR) sensor to allow the weapon to be used against surface targets. This addition was developed to provide ship defense against small vessel threats and other "floaters" in littoral waters, and to improve the weapon's performance against slower, low-flying aircraft. The FLIR's capability is also of use against low-observability missiles and can be linked with the RIM-116 Rolling Airframe Missile (RAM) system to increase

RAM engagement range and accuracy. The Block 1B also allows for an operator to visually identify and target threats. The system's technical features are as follows: weight, 13,600 pounds (Block 1B); dimensions of barrel length: Block 1, 59.8 inches, Block 1B, 78 inches; rate of fire, 3,000 to 4,500 rounds/min (selectable); muzzle velocity, 3,600 feet per second; magazine capacity, 1,550 rounds; caliber, 20 mm (20 × 102 mm); ammunition, Armor Piercing Discarding Sabot; ammunition stowage, 1,550 rounds; elevation, Block 0 = −10°/+80°, Block 1 = −20°/+80°, and Block 1B = −25°/+85°; traverse, −150° to +150°; effective range, 2.23 miles; and guidance system, Ku-band radar and forward-looking infrared.

The Close-In Weapons System is test-fired from the deck of the guided-missile cruiser USS *Monterey* (CG-61). *Monterey* and the *Theodore Roosevelt* Carrier Strike Group 8 were conducting operations in the US 5th Fleet area of responsibility in late 2008. *US Navy, Mass Communication Specialist 3rd Class William Weiner*

USS *Nimitz* Data	
Ordered	1967
Laid down	June 22, 1968
Launched	May 13, 1972
Commissioned	May 3, 1975
Builder	Newport News Shipbuilding
Class	*Nimitz*
Sponsor	Catherine Nimitz Lay
Displacement, standard	78,280 tons
Displacement, full	101,196 tons
Length, water	1,040 feet, line, full load
Length, hull	n.a.
Length	1,092 feet, flight deck
Length, overall	1,115 feet
Beam, waterline	134 feet
Beam, maximum	252 feet
Design draft maximum navigational	36.8 feet; limit: 41 feet
Endurance unlimited distance	20–25 years, at 30+ knots
Reactors	2 × Westinghouse A4W nuclear reactors
Machinery	4 × steam turbines
Speed	30+ knots
Armor	2.5-inch Kevlar over vital spaces
Armament, as built	3 × 8 NATO Sea Sparrow mounts, four Phalanx Close-In Weapon Systems, and four Rolling Airframe Missile (RAM) mounts
Radar	one tridimensional SPS-48E air search radar, one bidimensional SPS-49(V)5 air search radar, one SPS-67(V)1 surface search radar, one Mark 23 Target Acquisition System, six Mark 95 Missile Fire Control systems, one SPS-64(V)9 navigation radar, one Furuno 900 navigation radar, and one AN/SPN-44 landing approaching radar
Aircraft	approximately 60+
Aviation gasoline	2–2.7 million US gallons (JP-5)
Aviation facilities	four elevators, one flight deck, one hangar deck, four catapults
Crew	ship's company, 3,000–3,200; air wing, 1,500; other, 500

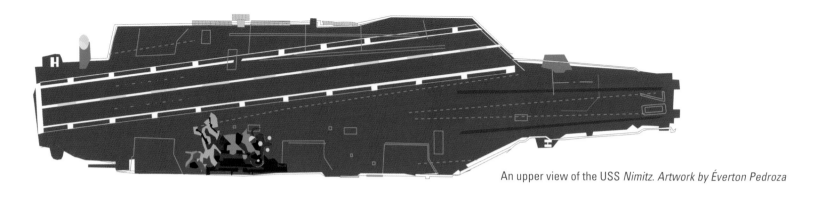
An upper view of the USS *Nimitz. Artwork by Éverton Pedroza*

A front view of the USS *Nimitz. Artwork by Éverton Pedroza*

A side view of the USS *Nimitz. Artwork by Éverton Pedroza*
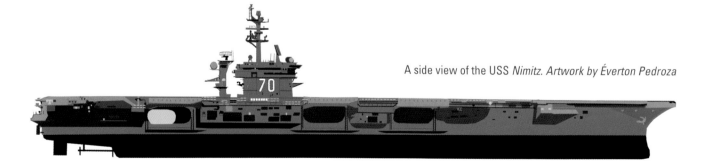

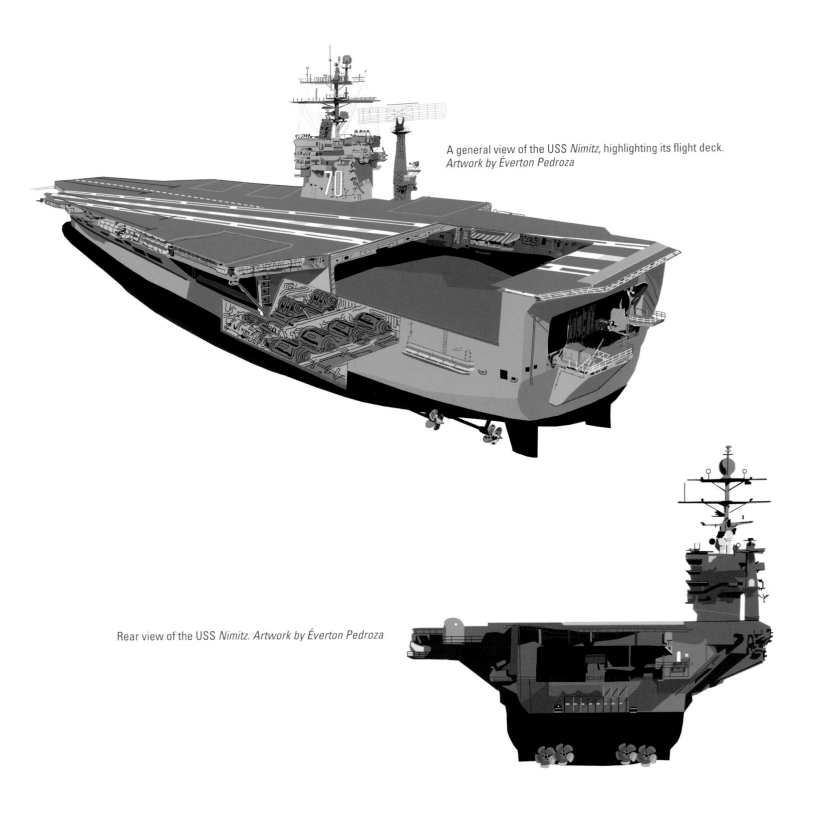

A general view of the USS *Nimitz,* highlighting its flight deck.
Artwork by Éverton Pedroza

Rear view of the USS *Nimitz. Artwork by Éverton Pedroza*

CHAPTER 2
Commissioning and the First Cruise

The USS *Nimitz* departing Norfolk, Virginia, circa early 1975. *US Navy*

Following its formal acceptance by the US Navy on April 11, 1975, the USS *Nimitz* received an aircraft aboard for the first time three days later, when a Grumman C-1A Trader cargo aircraft, "Salt One," piloted by Capt. Bryan W. Compton, performed the first arrested landing on that carrier.

On May 3, 1975, President Gerald R. Ford officially placed the USS *Nimitz* in commission.

The first port visit after commission, to Ft. Lauderdale, Florida, occurred on June 6–9, 1975. An initial refresher training period, prior to its inaugural cruise, took place at Guantanamo Bay, Cuba, from mid-July to mid-August of that year.

On August 14, the USS *Nimitz* sailed toward its first foreign deployment in northern Europe (Germany, Scotland, and England) as part of TASK FORCE '75 (also known as Nuclear Task Group 75), made up of the nuclear-powered, guided-missile-armed cruiser USS *South Carolina* (CGN-37), and the nuclear attack submarine USS *Seahorse* (SSN-669).

Carrier Air Wing 8 (CVW-8) was aboard CVN-68, comprising the following units: VMFA-333 "Shamrocks" and VF-74 "Bedevilers," both flying the McDonnell Douglas F-4J Phantom II; VA-82 "Marauders" and VA-86 "Sidewinders,"

The USS *Nimitz* replenishes from USS *Mount Baker* (AE-34) during UNREP training in Guantánamo Operations Area, Caribbean, July 31, 1975. *US Navy*

An LTV A-7E Corsair II prepares to be launched from the USS *Nimitz*. *US Navy*

A Grumman EA-6B Prowler seconds before being launched. *US Navy*

USS *Nimitz* and USS *South Carolina* operating in the North Atlantic, August 21, 1975. *US Navy*

The USS *Nimitz* enters the port of Wilhelmshaven, Germany, for a visit, August 27, 1975. *US Navy*

both with the LTV A-7E Corsair II; VA-35 "Black Panthers," equipped with the A-6E and KA-6D Intruder; VAQ-130 "Zappers," flying the Grumman EA-6B Prowler; RVAH-9 "Hoot Owls," with North American RA-5C Vigilante; VAW-116 "Sun Kings," equipped with the Grumman E-2B Hawkeye; and, finally, the HC-2 "Fleet Angels," flying the Sikorsky SH-3G Sea King. Also present on that cruise were the VRC-40 "Rawhides," equipped with the Grumman C-1A Trader, and the HS-15 "Red Lions," flying Sikorsky SH-3H Sea King. A detachment of VF-31 "Tomcatters," equipped with F-4J Phantom IIs, was also part of CVW-8 for that USS *Nimitz* initial cruise.

USS *Nimitz* and USS *South Carolina* departed from Naval Station Norfolk, Virginia, on August 19, 1975, and gathered five days later with USS *Seahorse* at sea.

Ports of call included Wilhelmshaven/Bremerhaven in (then) West Germany, Edinburgh, Scotland, and Portsmouth, England.

Exercises were then conducted with the West Germans, NATO's Standing Naval Force, and with the Royal Navy and the Royal Air Force, in Exercise NIMEX.

Nimitz and *South Carolina* arrived back to Norfolk on September 15, 1975.

With rails manned, the USS *Nimitz* enters Wilhelmshaven Harbor, Germany, for a port visit, August 27, 1975. *US Navy*

USS *Nimitz* and HMS *Ark Royal* berthed at the Norfolk Naval Base, Virginia, in April 1976. They are dressed with flags in honor of the birthday of Queen Juliana of the Netherlands. *US Navy*

A Soviet Tupolev Tu-142 maritime recconnaissance aircraft is escorted by a VF-74 F-4J "Phantom" fighter as it flies past USS *Nimitz*, July 15, 1976. *US Navy*

HMS *Blake* (C-99) and USS *Nimitz* (CVN-68) operate in the English Channel during an exercise, October 4, 1975. *US Navy*

CHAPTER 3
Operation Evening Light

In January 1980 the USS *Nimitz*, along with the USS *California* (also known as CGN-36, the lead ship of the *California*-class of nuclear-powered guided-missile cruisers) and USS *Texas* (or CGN-39, the second *Virginia*-class nuclear-powered guided-missile cruiser), were dispatched to the Indian Ocean area in order to reinforce the US Navy presence in that operational theater amid the crisis unleashed by the Islamic Revolution in Iran, which happened between January 1978 and February 1979 and caused the overthrow of a dynasty led by Mohammad Reza Pahlevi, a traditional US ally, and the founding of a republic ruled by Islamic laws.

As an additional result, in November 1979, members of the Muslim Student Followers of the Imam's Line, who supported the Iranian Revolution, invaded the US embassy in Tehran and took its employees as hostages, starting a tension that lasted for 444 days and included a couple of rescue attempts.

The first of these, christened Operation Eagle Claw / Operation Evening Light, involved all the branches of the armed forces. It was conceived as a two-phase plan: in the first stage, some aircraft would fly to a position within the Iranian desert coded as "Desert One," which would be secured and supplied with fuel provided by Lockheed C-130 transports until the second phase, which would consist of the arrival of the rescue forces. They would be lifted to another position, "Desert Two," by means of eight Sikorsky RH-53D Sea Stallion helicopters. From there the rescue teams would reach Tehran by land. Other teams would disable the electrical power there, then take an air base and a stadium where the hostages and rescue teams would be gathered and from which they would be taken to the air base already under control by US forces. Lockheed C-141 cargo aircraft would bring all those involved back to the US.

Apart from being the base from which the Sea Stallions would depart, the USS *Nimitz*'s Carrier Air Wing 8 was put in charge of the air coverage for the operation (augmented by Carrier Air Wing 14 aboard the USS *Coral Sea*). By that time, CVW-8 was made up of the following units: VF-41 "Black Aces" and VF-84 "Jolly Rogers," both flying the Grumman F-1A Tomcat; VA-82 "Marauders" and VA-86 "Sidewinders," both equipped with LTV A-7E Corsair II; VA-35 "Black Panthers," flying the Grumman A-6E Intruder and KA-6D; VFP-63 Det. 5 "Eyes of the Fleet," with the LTV RF-8G Crusader; VAQ-134 "Garudas," flying the Grumman EA-6B Prowler; VS-24 "Scouts," with the Lockheed S-3A Viking; HS-9 "Sea Griffins," equipped with the Sikorksy SH-3H Sea King; and VAW-112 "Golden Hawks," flying the Grumman E-2B Hawkeye. Other provisional units aboard the USS *Nimitz* were embarked due to the Iranian crisis only, since it was the case of the HM-16 Det. "Seahawks," with its Sea Stallions; the VQ-1 Det. B "World Watchers," equipped with the Douglas EA-3B "Skywarrior"; and the VRC-50 Det. "Foo Dogs," flying the Grumman C-2A Greyhound. For the operation, CVW-8's Tomcats and Corsairs received red and black stripes over their right wings, in order make them easier to distinguish from the Iranian aircraft if air combat were to happen.

However, as is well documented, the operation, unleashed on April 24, 1980, resulted in a total failure when still at its very early stage, dictated by a sequence of events of multiple natures, including meteorological. The consequences were the loss of eight US servicemen (and four wounded). One helicopter and one transport aircraft were also lost, while another five Sea Stallions were abandoned in the Iranian desert.

Task Force 70, January 23, 1980. The USS *Midway*, USS *Kitty Hawk,* and USS *Nimitz* during the Iranian hostage crisis. *Edward F. Bronson Collection via US Navy*

Front to back, an aerial view of the aircraft carriers USS *Kitty Hawk* and USS *Midway*, and the nuclear-powered aircraft carrier USS *Nimitz*, somewhere in the Indian Ocean. Escort ships accompany the carriers. *PH3 Lee Schnell–US Navy*

Grumman F-14A Tomcats operated by the VF-41 and VF-84 squadrons aboard the USS *Nimitz* during the Iranian hostage crisis. *US Navy*

Some RH-53 Sea Stallion helicopters are being readied in the hangar of the USS *Nimitz* prior to Operation Evening Light. *US Navy photo by PH1 K. D. Homedale*

A tow tractor moves an RH-53 Sea Stallion helicopter into position on the flight deck of the nuclear-powered aircraft carrier USS *Nimitz* prior to the start of Operation Evening Light. *US Navy*

Three RH-53 Sea Stallion helicopters are lined up on the flight deck of the nuclear-powered aircraft carrier USS *Nimitz* in preparation for Operation Evening Light. *US Navy*

Another view of the Sea Stallions prior to departure for Operation Evening Light. *US Navy*

Operation Evening Light, a rescue mission to Iran, gets underway as an RH-53 Sea Stallion helicopter lifts off the flight deck of the nuclear-powered aircraft carrier USS *Nimitz*. Additional helicopters are also lined up to be launched. *US Navy*

As for the USS *Nimitz*, it returned to its home base in late May 1980, while the last hostage was released in November 1982.

However, that year would not come to an end without the release of *Final Countdown*, a science fiction movie that came to theaters in August 1980, having been filmed aboard the USS *Nimitz*. The plot takes CVN-68 back to a time before the Japanese imperial navy's attack on Pearl Harbor, after the USS *Nimitz* had crossed something like a dimensional portal. The dogfight scenes between the carrier's F-14s and the Mitsubishi A6M Zero fighters are among the movie's high points.

A right-side view of RH-53D Sea Stallion helicopters in flight, just after lifting off the flight deck of the USS *Nimitz*. Destination: Operation Evening Light, Iran. *US Navy*

A left-side view of RH-35D Sea Stallion helicopters in flight heading to Operation Evening Light, Iran. *US Navy*

CHAPTER 4
When the *Nimitz* Hit the News

The Gulf of Sidra Incident

Following its involvement in the Iranian hostage crisis, the USS *Nimitz* would see new action in August 1981, in what became known as the "Gulf of Sidra Incident." Actually, it was the latest (by that time) confrontation in a series of tensions between US and Libyan forces, whose first combat occurred on March 21, 1973. Libyan interceptors fired missiles at a C-130 cargo plane after the latter flew inside a "restricted area" that Libya had created within a 100-mile radius of Tripoli. Slightly more than seven years later, on September 16, 1980, Libyan planes attacked a US reconnaissance aircraft.

However, on August 12–14, 1981, the US government officially announced it would hold naval exercises some days later. The maneuvers, called "Open Ocean Missile-X," would comprise missile tests and exercise the freedom of navigation in an area whose sovereignty was then claimed by Libya. For that deployment, the USS *Nimitz* departed from its home base at Naval Station Norfolk on August 3, 1981.

The naval component of such exercise was made up of two carrier battle groups: one led by the USS *Forrestal* (CV-59) and another one by the USS *Nimitz* and its Carrier Air Wing 8, which had almost the same composition as it had in the *Nimitz*'s previous cruise, apart from the following squadrons: VMAQ-2 Det. Y "Playboys," flying the aforementioned Grumman EA-6B Prowler, and the VAW-124 "Bear Aces," with the Grumman E-2C Hawkeye. The RF-8 Crusaders were not present on that cruise either.

The most famous event of the "Open Ocean Missile-X" took place on August 19, 1981, when two F-14s from VF-41 "Black Aces," coded as "Fast Eagle 102" and "Fast Eagle 107," were flying combat air patrol to cover another aircraft engaged in a missile exercise. One such aircraft was an S-3A Viking, which was flying

in a racetrack orbit inside Libya's claimed restricted area to try to provoke the Libyans to react. A VAW-124's E-2C alerted the Viking's crew that two Sukhoi Su-22 "Fitter" fighters had taken off from an air base near the city of Sirte and guided the Tomcats to intercept them, while the Viking maneuvered to evade the Libyan fighters. These opened fire with missiles against one of the F-14s, which managed to escape to the Libyan shot. This led the Tomcat crews to fire back in self-defense. As a result, the Libyan fighters were shot down and their pilots ejected. After the incident, some mock attacks with other Libyan MiGs were performed against the aircraft carrier, but without further aerial combats.

The USS *Nimitz* finally returned to its port in early February 1982, after having visited Naples, Italy; Tunis, Tunisia; Livorno, Italy; Haifa, Israel; and Palma de Maiorca, Spain.

On March 8, 1985, CVN-68 left its home port. Carrier Air Wing 8 was aboard, having been integrated by the following units: VF-41 "Black Aces" and VF-84 "Jolly Rogers," both equipped with the Grumman F-14A Tomcat; VA-86 "Sidewinders," equipped with LTV A-7E Corsair II; VA-35 "Black Panthers" and VA-82 "Marauders," both flying the Grumman A-6E Intruder; VAQ-138 "Yellow Jackets," with the Grumman EA-6B "Prowler"; VS-24 "Scouts," flying the Lockheed S-3B Viking; HS-9 "Sea Griffins," equipped with the Sikorsky SH-3H Sea King; VAW-124 "Bear Aces," flying the E-2C Hawkeye; and VQ-2, with the Douglas EA-3B Skywarrior.

The *Nimitz* Strike Force was made up of the nuclear-powered cruiser USS *South Carolina* (CGN-37), the guided-missile destroyer USS *Kidd* (DDG-100), and the USS *Kalamazoo* (AOR-6), a replenishment oiler.

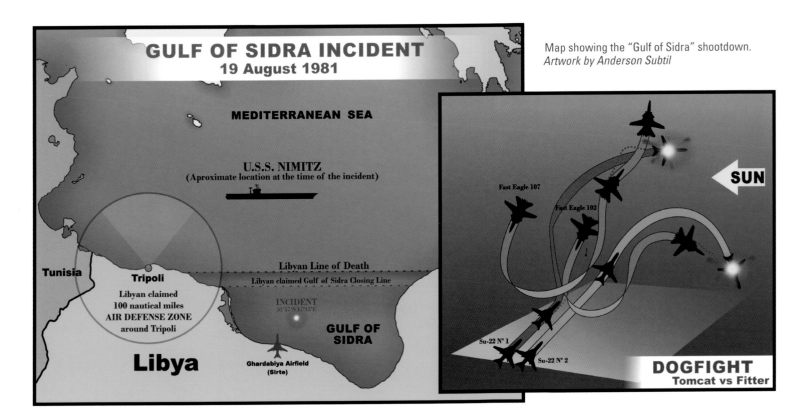

GULF OF SIDRA INCIDENT
19 August 1981

MEDITERRANEAN SEA

U.S.S. NIMITZ
(Aproximate location at the time of the incident)

Tunisia

Tripoli

Libyan claimed
100 nautical miles
AIR DEFENSE ZONE
around Tripoli

Libya

Ghardabiya Airfield
(Sirte)

Libyan Line of Death
Libyan claimed Gulf of Sidra Closing Line

INCIDENT
31°57'N 17°15'E

GULF OF
SIDRA

Fast Eagle 107

Fast Eagle 102

SUN

Su-22 N° 1

Su-22 N° 2

DOGFIGHT
Tomcat vs Fitter

Map showing the "Gulf of Sidra" shootdown.
Artwork by Anderson Subtil

TWA Flight 847

In mid-June 1985, the USS *Nimitz* was involved in a sui generis event when two Lebanese Shiite Muslim gunmen hijacked TWA Flight 847, carrying 153 passengers and crew, including many Americans. As a consequence, USS *Nimitz* canceled a visit to Livorno, Italy, and was ordered to steam at flank speed to the eastern Mediterranean, off the coast of Lebanon, where it remained until August 1985. During this period, the strike assets operated by CVW-8 executed bombing sorties against forces based in Beirut, Lebanon, who were linked to the terrorists who had taken the airliner.

USS *Nimitz* turned over to USS *Saratoga* (CV-60) at Augusta Bay, Italy, in early September, but the ongoing crisis in the Middle East in the wake of terrorists kidnapping several Americans in Beirut forced it to divert and race to eastern Mediterranean. Finally, on October 4, USS *Nimitz* returned to home port after a seven-month deployment.

Apart from the expected losses between its belligerent countries, the Iran-Iraq War, which commenced in 1980, also brought significant threat to the international oil commerce, since the Iranian forces began to attack Kuwaiti and Saudi ships that carried much of the crude oil produced in the Iraqi plants.

Operation Earnest Will

As an effort to protect those ships (which were reflagged as being of US origin), USS *Nimitz* left its home base in Bremerton on September 2, 1988, and reached the North Arabian Sea on October 29 to take part in Operation Earnest Will, planned to protect shipping lanes. For that deployment (the *Nimitz*'s eighth since it was commissioned), CVN-68 had embarked Carrier Air Wing 9, which comprised the following squadrons: VAQ-138 "Yellow Jacket," equipped with the Grumman EA-6B Prowler; VAW-112 "Golden Hawks," flying the Grumman E-2C Hawkeye; VA-146 "Blue Diamonds," with the LTV A-7E Corsair II; VS-33 "Screwbirds," equipped with the Lockheed S-3A Viking; HS-2 "Golden Falcons," with the Sikorsky SH-3H Sea King; VA-165 "Boomers," flying the Grumman A-6 Intruder; VF-211 "Checkmates" and VF-24 "Fighting Renegades," both equipped with the Grumman F-14A Tomcat; and, finally, the VA-147 "Argonauts," flying the LTV A-7E Corsair II.

For Operation Earnest Will, during which the USS *Nimitz* acted to protect eleven oil ships, it relieved the USS *Carl Vinson* and eventually headed back toward its home port, where it arrived in early March 1989.

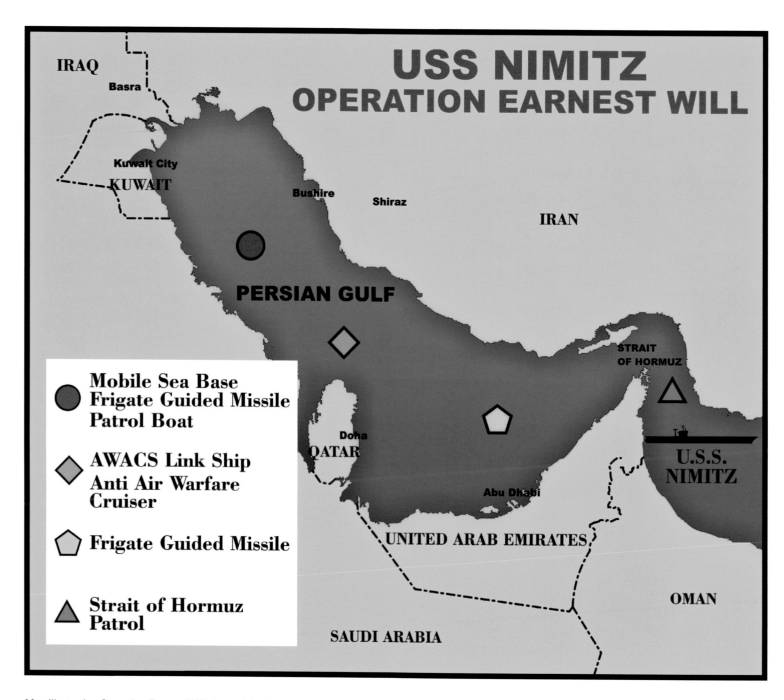

USS NIMITZ
OPERATION EARNEST WILL

Legend:

- ● Mobile Sea Base Frigate Guided Missile Patrol Boat
- ◆ AWACS Link Ship Anti Air Warfare Cruiser
- ⬠ Frigate Guided Missile
- ▲ Strait of Hormuz Patrol

IRAQ
Basra
Kuwait City
KUWAIT
Bushire
Shiraz
IRAN
PERSIAN GULF
STRAIT OF HORMUZ
Doha
QATAR
U.S.S. NIMITZ
Abu Dhabi
UNITED ARAB EMIRATES
OMAN
SAUDI ARABIA

Map illustrating Operation Earnest Will. *Artwork by Anderson Subtil*

Operation Desert Shield/Storm

The unexpected invasion of Kuwait by Iraqi forces in August 1990 led to the formation of a coalition of countries intended to expel those forces from the Kuwaiti territory.

That effort was planned to be achieved by means of a two-phase operation: Desert Shield (intended to improve the readiness of all the Allied forces then based in Saudi Arabia and other countries surrounding the invader forces) and Desert Storm (made up of all the combat actions against Saddam Hussein's military contingents in Kuwait).

For that deployment, the USS *Nimitz* left Bremerton, Washington, and headed toward the Western Pacific and Arabian Gulf in late February 1991. CVW-9 was aboard the vessel again with the same organization, except for VA-146 and VA-147 squadrons, which had traded their Corsairs for F/A-18C Hornets and were renamed as VFAs, to make evident their recently added fighter capabilities. For "Desert Storm," CVN-68 relieved the USS *Ranger* (CV-61).

The USS *Nimitz* arrived in the Arabian Gulf on April 18, 1991, and immediately commenced combat air patrol missions to support Desert Storm operations. When it left that combat theater on July 13, 1991, CVN-68's aircraft had been responsible for more than 12,000 flight hours. It is worth noting that the Grumman E-2C+ Hawkeye Plus made its maiden deployment during this cruise.

Following the planned course for that cruise, the USS *Nimitz* sailed toward Pattaya Beach, Thailand; Hong Kong; and Pearl Harbor, Hawaii, and finally came back to its home port in Bremerton in late August 1991.

On February 19, 1993, the USS *Nimitz* departed Bremerton for another operational cruise. Carrier Air Wing 9 (CVW-9) was aboard, then composed of the following squadrons: VF-211 "Fighting Checkmates" and VF-24 "Fighting Renegades," both flying the Grumman F-14A Tomcat; VFA-146 "Blue Diamonds" and VFA-147 "Argonauts," both equipped with the McDonnell Douglas F/A-18C Hornet; VA-165 "Boomers," flying the attack (A-6E) and tanker (KA-6D) versions of the Grumman A-6 Intruder; VAQ-138 "Yellow Jackets," with the Grumman EA-6B; VS-33 "Screwbirds," flying the Lockheed S-3A Viking; and, finally, the HS-2 "Golden Falcons," equipped with the Sikorsky HH-60/SH-60H/F Seahawk. The airborne early-warning and control duties were under the responsibilities of the VAW-112 "Golden Hawks" and their Grumman E-2C Hawkeyes. CVW-9 was part of Carrier Group 7.

For that cruise, the *Nimitz* battle group was also composed of the USS *Truxtun* (CGN-35), a guided-missile/nuclear-powered cruiser, and by the conventionally powered cruiser USS *Chancellorsville*, which collectively made up Destroyer Squadron 23. The battle group's area of operations comprised the Western Pacific, the Indian Ocean, and the Arabian Gulf.

Operation Southern Watch

Between late March and July 1993, when it relieved USS *Kitty Hawk*, CVN-68 became involved in Operation Southern Watch when it entered the Strait of Hormuz. That operation commenced in August 1992 as an Allied effort to stop the aggressions perpetrated by the Iraqi regime against the Shiite Muslims in southern Iraq.

After having launched hundreds of missions against their targets, which included air bases and ground-based air defense systems, the USS *Nimitz* was relieved by the USS *Abraham Lincoln* in early July 1993 and sailed toward Puget Sound Naval Shipyard, where it arrived on August 1, 1993. Before it reached its final destination, the locations visited by the USS *Nimitz* during that cruise were Hong Kong, Singapore, Jebel Ali (United Arab Emirates), Pattaya Beach (Thailand), Pearl Harbor, and North Island.

Operation Enduring Freedom

As a direct consequence of the terrorist attacks against the World Trade Center on September, 11, 2001, the US government unleashed Operation Enduring Freedom (OEF).

For the USS *Nimitz*, the OEF commenced in May 2007, when its embarked Carrier Air Wing 11 (CVW-11) was charged with providing close airpower support and reconnaissance to International Security Assistance Force (ISAF) troops on the ground in Afghanistan.

CVW-11 comprised the VFA-14 "Tophatters" (with Boeing F/A-18E Super Hornet), VFA-41 "Black Aces" (flying the F/A-18F Super Hornets in addition to the E model), VFA-81 "Sunliners" (still flying the F/A-18C Hornet as of then), VAW-117 "Wallbangers" (with Grumman E-2C Hawkeye), VMFA-232 "Red Devils" (equipped with the same aircraft as the VFA-81), VAQ-135 "Black Ravens" (flying the Grumman EA-6B Prowler), VRC-30 "Providers" (with the C-2 Greyhound), and HS-6 "Indians" (with the Sikorsky Seahawks).

For that deployment, CVN-68 had left its home port of San Diego the previous month, being the flagship of the *Nimitz* Strike Group, made up of the guided-missile cruiser USS *Princeton* (CG-59) and guided-missile destroyers USS *John Paul Jones* (DDG-53), USS *Higgins* (DDG-76), USS *Chafee* (DDG-90), and USS *Pinckney* (DDG-91). The HSL-49 "Scorpions" and HSL-37 "Easy Riders," flying the antisubmarine versions of the Sikorsky Blackhawk helicopter, were also part of the strike force. All those ships made up Task Force 58.

Until late July of that year, CVW-11 launched more than 2,653 sorties totaling more than 8,240 flight hours. Of these, 835 sorties and 4,697 flight hours were in direct support of Allied ground-based combat forces.

An EA-6B Prowler assigned to the VAQ-142 "Gray Wolves" prepares to launch from the aircraft carrier USS *Nimitz* to support Operation Enduring Freedom. *US Navy photo by Mass Communication Specialist 3rd Class Raul Moreno Jr.*

Different moments showing the preparation and launching of Hornet and Super Hornet fighters from the USS *Nimitz* during Operation Enduring Freedom. *US Navy photos*

An F/A-18C Hornet assigned to the "Death Rattlers" of Marine Fighter Attack Squadron (VMFA) 323 launches from the USS *Nimitz* to support Operation Enduring Freedom. Note the different color deck crew vests: yellow vests are worn by aircraft directors; blue vests are worn by aircraft handlers, elevator and tractors operators; green vests are used by those responsible for heavy duties such as cargo handling, aircraft maintenance and ship's catapult and arresting gear; purple vests are worn by those responsible for handle fuels; red vests are used by weapons specialists; brown vests are worn by "Plane Captains," who oversee the general status of a given aircraft within a squadron. Finally, white vests are used by those who can act as safety observers, squadron plane inspectors, and landing signal officers, although they also can perform other tasks such as medical functions. *US Navy photo by Mass Communication Specialist 3rd Class Raul Moreno Jr.*

An F/A-18C Hornet assigned to the "Death Rattlers" of Marine Fighter Attack Squadron (VMFA) 323 prepares to launch from the USS *Nimitz* to support Operation Enduring Freedom. *US Navy photo by Mass Communication Specialist 3rd Class Raul Moreno Jr.*

An F/A-18C Hornet assigned to the "Death Rattlers" of Marine Fighter Attack Squadron (VMFA) 323 prepares to launch from the USS *Nimitz* in support of Operation Enduring Freedom. *US Navy photo by Mass Communication Specialist 3rd Class Raul Moreno Jr.*

An F/A-18E Super Hornet assigned to the "Blue Diamonds" of Strike Fighter Squadron (VFA) 146 launches the USS *Nimitz* in support of Operation Enduring Freedom. *US Navy photo by Mass Communication Specialist 3rd Class Raul Moreno Jr.*

An F/A-18E Super Hornet assigned to the "Blue Diamonds" of Strike Fighter Squadron (VFA) 146 launches from the USS *Nimitz* in support of Operation Enduring Freedom. *US Navy photo by Mass Communication Specialist 3rd Class Raul Moreno Jr.*

An F/A-18F Super Hornet assigned to the Black Knights of Strike Fighter Squadron (VFA) 154 launches from the flight deck of the USS *Nimitz* during Operation Enduring Freedom. *US Navy photo by Mass Communication Specialist 3rd Class Raul Moreno Jr.*

Gulf of Oman, July 15, 2013. An F/A-18F Super Hornet assigned to the "Black Knights" of Strike Fighter Squadron (VFA) 154 launches from the flight deck of the USS *Nimitz* during Operation Enduring Freedom. *US Navy photo by Mass Communication Specialist 3rd Class Raul Moreno Jr.*

An F/A-18C Hornet assigned to the "Death Rattlers" of Marine Fighter Attack Squadron (VMFA) 323 prepares to launch from the flight deck of the USS *Nimitz* during Operation Enduring Freedom. *US Navy photo by Mass Communication Specialist 3rd Class Raul Moreno Jr.*

An F/A-18E Super Hornet assigned to the "Argonauts" of Strike Fighter Squadron (VFA) 147 launches from the flight deck of the USS *Nimitz* during Operation Enduring Freedom. *US Navy photo by Mass Communication Specialist 3rd Class Raul Moreno Jr.*

Gulf of Oman, June 13, 2013. An F/A-18E Super Hornet assigned to the "Argonauts" of Strike Fighter Squadron (VFA) 147 prepares to takeoff from the USS *Nimitz* during the first day of combat flight operations for *Nimitz'* current deployment. *US Navy photo by Mass Communication Specialist 3rd Class Nathan R. McDonald*

An F/A-18E Super Hornet assigned to the "Argonauts" of Strike Fighter Squadron (VFA) 147 launches from the flight deck of the USS *Nimitz* during Operation Enduring Freedom. *US Navy photo by Mass Communication Specialist 3rd Class Raul Moreno Jr.*

An E-2C from the VAW-117 "Wallbangers" squadron goes through maintenance, launch, and recovery from the USS *Nimitz* during Operation Enduring Freedom. *US Navy*

An E-2C from the VAW-117 "Wallbangers" squadron goes through maintenance, launch, and recovery from the USS *Nimitz* during Operation Enduring Freedom. *US Navy*

Marines assigned to the VMFA-323 "Death Rattlers" move ordnance on the flight deck of the aircraft carrier USS *Nimitz*. *US Navy photo by Mass Communication Specialist 3rd Class Raul Moreno Jr.*

Gulf of Oman, July 12, 2013. Sailors fight a simulated fire during a general-quarters drill aboard the aircraft carrier USS *Nimitz* as part of Operation Enduring Freedom. *US Navy photo by MCS3 Raul Moreno Jr.*

Gulf of Oman, July 13, 2013. The aircraft carrier USS *Nimitz* transits alongside the Military Sealift Command dry cargo and ammunition ship USNS *Alan Shepard* (center) and the guided-missile destroyer USS *William P. Lawrence* during a replenishment at sea while participating in Operation Enduring Freedom. *US Navy photo by MCS3 Raul Moreno Jr.*

The aircraft carrier USS *Nimitz* conducts a replenishment at sea, this time with the Military Sealift Command fast combat support ship USNS *Rainier* during Operation Enduring Freedom. *US Navy photo by Mass Communication Specialist 3rd Class Raul Moreno Jr.*

The aircraft carrier USS *Nimitz* pulls into Jebel Ali for a port visit as part of Operation Enduring Freedom. *US Navy photo by MCS3 Raul Moreno Jr.*

An F/A-18E Super Hornet assigned to the VFA-147 "Argonauts" launches from the flight deck of the aircraft carrier USS *Nimitz* during Operation Enduring Freedom. *US Navy photo by MCS3 Raul Moreno Jr.*

Sailors place weather guards over a catapult on the flight deck of the aircraft carrier USS *Nimitz* while supporting missions for Operation Enduring Freedom. *US Navy photo by MCS3 Raul Moreno Jr.*

Operation Iraqi Freedom

On April 9, 2003, the US Navy announced that USS *Nimitz* would replace the USS *Abraham Lincoln* in the ongoing Operation Iraqi Freedom, authorized when Iraq was accused of violation of the UN Security Council–adopted Resolution 1441, which "prohibits stockpiling and importing weapons of mass destruction."

The aerial operations for that deployment were performed by Carrier Air Wing 11 (CVW-11), made up of the following squadrons: VFA-14 Strike Fighter Squadron 14 "Tophatters," flying the Boeing F-18E Super Hornet; VFA-41 Strike Fighter Squadron 41 "Black Aces," equipped with the Boeing F-18F Super Hornet; VFA-86 Strike Fighter Squadron 86 "Sidewinders," flying the Boeing F/A-18C Hornet; VFA-97 Strike Fighter Squadron 97 "Warhawks," initially with the Boeing F/A-18A Hornet, which was replaced by the "C" model from 2004 until 2012; VAW-117 Carrier Airborne Early Warning Squadron 117 "Wallbangers," flying the Grumman E-2C Hawkeye; VAQ-135 Electronic Attack Squadron 135 "Black Ravens," equipped with Grumman EA-6B Prowler; VRC-30 Fleet Logistics Support Squadron 30 "Providers," with Grumman C-2 Greyhound; and HS-6 Helicopter Anti-Submarine Squadron 6 "Indians," flying the Sikorsky MH-60S Seahawk.

The USS *Nimitz* Carrier Strike Group (CSG) replaced the USS *Carl Vinson* CSG in the Persian Gulf on July 5, 2005. The USS *Theodore Roosevelt* CSG arrived on station to replace the USS *Nimitz* CSG on September 24, 2005.

The aircraft operated by CVW-11 onboard the *Nimitz* during that deployment logged a high amount of flying hours and operational

Central Command area of responsibility, June 28, 2003. USS *Nimitz* conducts flight operations as part of its mission for Operation Iraqi Freedom. *US Navy photo by Photographer's Mate 3rd Class Elizabeth Thompson*

Seahawk helicopters from the HSM-75 squadron fly ahead of the USS *Nimitz* during Operation Iraqi Freedom. *US Navy photo by MC2(SW) Jason Behnke*

An F/A-18F Super Hornet is about to touch the flight deck of the USS *Nimitz*, then deployed in support of Operation Iraqi Freedom. *US Navy photo by Photographer's Mate 3rd Class Kristi Earl*

The Arabian Gulf, April 15, 2003. USS *Nimitz*, USS *Princeton*, and USS *Bridge* participate in an underway replenishment. *Nimitz* Carrier Strike Force and Carrier Air Wing 11 were then deployed in support of Operation Iraqi Freedom. *US Navy photo by Photographer's Mate 3rd Class Kristi Earl*

Central Command area of responsibility, September 6, 2003. USS *Nimitz* sails through the Indian Ocean during Operation Iraqi Freedom, the multinational coalition effort to end the regime of Saddam Hussein. *US Navy photo by Photographer's Mate 2nd Class Monica L. McLaughlin*

The USS *Nimitz*, with its crew and many of its aircraft on the flight deck, navigates during Operation Iraqi Freedom. *US Navy*

The Arabian Gulf, April 8, 2003. USS *Nimitz* and Carrier Air Wing 11 carry out flight operations in support of Operation Iraqi Freedom, the multi-national coalition effort to liberate the Iraqi people, and end the regime of Saddam Hussein. *US Navy photo by Photographer's Mate 3rd Class Kristi Earl*

The USS *Nimitz* participates in air operations in the Arabian Gulf as part of Operation Iraqi Freedom. *US Navy photo by Photographer's Mate 3rd Class Kristi J. Earl*

The USS *Nimitz* resupplies during Operation Iraqi Freedom. *US Navy*

The Arabian Gulf, April 17, 2003. A group of sailors participate in the daily FOD walkdown aboard USS *Nimitz* at the time of Operation Iraqi Freedom. *US Navy photo by PHAN Shannon Renfroe*

At sea aboard USS *Nimitz*, March 27, 2003. Aircraft from Carrier Air Wing 11 are chocked and chained to the forward catapults, while the USS *Princeton* sails by. *Nimitz* and its battle group were then forward deployed conducting missions in support of Operation Iraqi Freedom. *US Navy Photo by AN Maebel Tinoko*

At sea aboard USS *Nimitz* on March 24, 2003, Aviation Ordnanceman 3rd Class Joshua Young of Cincinnati, Ohio, uses a forklift to move a Blue 110 (1,000-lb. bomb). *Nimitz* was then deployed in support of Operation Iraqi Freedom. *US Navy photo by PH3 Kristi J. Earl*

A sailor maintains ordnance ready for use onboard the USS *Nimitz* during Operation Iraqi Freedom. *US Navy photo by MCS3 Raul Moreno Jr.*

The Arabian Gulf, April 13, 2003. Aviation ordnancemen of the VFA-14 "Top Hatters" attach ordnance onto an F/A-18 Super Hornet on the flight deck aboard USS *Nimitz*, during Operation Iraqi Freedom. *US Navy photo by PHAN Timothy F. Sosa*

Arabian Gulf, April 18, 2003. An aviation ordnanceman lifts an AIM-120 missile to load it onto an aircraft onboard the USS *Nimitz*. *Nimitz* and its embarked Carrier Air Wing 11 were then deployed in support of Operation Iraqi Freedom. *US Navy photo by Photographer's Mate 3rd Class Yesenia Rosas*

An E-2C Hawkeye from the VAW-117 "Wallbangers" comes in for an arrested landing on the flight deck of USS *Nimitz* during Operation Iraqi Freedom. *US Navy photo by Angel G. Hilbrands*

An F/A-18C Hornet of the VFA-94 "Mighty Strikes" prepares to take off from one of four steam-driven catapults on the flight deck of USS *Nimitz,* then deployed and en route to the Persian Gulf in support of Operation Iraqi Freedom. *US Navy photo by Photographer's Mate 3rd Class Yesenia Rosas*

An F/A-18F Super Hornet from the VFA-14 "Top Hatters" prepares to take off from one of four steam-powered catapults during night flight operations on the flight deck of USS *Nimitz* as part of Operation Iraqi Freedom. *US Navy photo by Photographer's Mate 3rd Class Yesenia Rosas*

A Flight Deck Shooter launches an F/A-18F Super Hornet from the VFA-41 "Black Aces" off one of the four steam-powered catapults on the flight deck of the USS *Nimitz* during Operation Iraqi Freedom. *US Navy photo by Photographer's Mate 3rd Class Yesenia Rosas*

Late July 2003. An F/A-18F Super Hornet from the VFA-41 "Black Aces" completes an arrested landing on the flight deck of USS *Nimitz. Nimitz* Strike Force and Carrier Air Wing 11 were then deployed in support of Operation Iraqi Freedom. *US Navy photo by Photographer's Mate 3rd Class Yesenia Rosas*

Late August 2003. Various Navy aircraft are chocked and chained to the flight deck, as the guided-missile cruiser USS *Princeton* (CG-59) steams forward of USS *Nimitz* (CVN-68) during Operation Iraqi Freedom. *US Navy photo by Airman Maebel Tinoko*

Early September 2003. On the flight deck of the USS *Nimitz*, Carrier Air Wing 11 aircraft are strategically parked during a scheduled no-fly day as part of Operation Iraqi Freedom. *US Navy photo by Airman Angel G Hilbrands*

San Diego, California, November 5, 2003. The USS *Nimitz* returns home to family and friends after an eight-month deployment in support of Operation Iraqi Freedom. *US Navy photo by Photographer's Mate Airman Rebecca J. Moat, Fleet Imaging Command Pacific*

Another shot of the USS *Nimitz* coming home after Operation Iraqi Freedom. *US Navy photo by Photographer's Mate Airman Rebecca J. Moat, Fleet Imaging Command Pacific*

sorties: the VFA-14's Hornets accumulated over 2,100 sorties and logged over 4,300 hours, while the VAW-117's Hawkeyes flew about 500 sorties (194 of them while in direct support of Operation Sea Dragon III, a component of Operation Iraqi Freedom).

In September 2009, the USS *Nimitz* returned to the same area of operations when it relieved the USS *Ronald Reagan* CSG and became the flagship of Task Force 50.

Carrier Air Wing 11's formation remained almost the same, but it was joined by other units, such as the VFA-97 "Warhawks" and the VFA-86 "Sidewinders," both flying the F/A-18C Hornet.

When it completed its tour in December that year, CVW-11 had flown over 2,623 combat sorties distributed over 15,000 flight hours.

For that deployment, the USS *Nimitz* was accompanied by Destroyer Squadron 23 (DESRON-23) and the USS *Chosin* cruiser (CG-65). Ships assigned to DESRON-23 included USS *Pinckney* (DDG-91), USS *Sampson* (DDG-102), and the frigate USS *Rentz* (FFG-46).

The USS *Nimitz* contributed to the Allied efforts for Operation Enduring Freedom during the spring of 2013, when its CVW-11 flew 1,374 combat sorties in direct support of ground troops. The air wing also participated in contingency operations in the Red Sea in response to the Syrian chemical-weapons crisis.

On March 29, 2013, CVN-68 left its home port of Naval Station Everett, Washington, to join the guided missile cruiser USS *Princeton* (CG-59) for a previously scheduled Western Pacific deployment. For that deployment, the USS *Nimitz* embarked with Carrier Air Wing 11 (CVW-11), made up of the following squadrons: VAQ-142 "Gray Wolves" (flying the Grumman EA-6B Prowler), VAW-117 "Wallbangers" (equipped with the Grumman E-2C Hawkeye), VFA-146 "Blue Diamonds" (with the Boeing F/A-18C Hornet), VFA-147 "Jason and Argonauts" (equipped with the F/A-18E Super Hornet), VFA-154 "Black Knights (flying the F/A-18F Super Hornet), VMFA-323 "Death Rattlers" (with the F/A-18C), HSC-6 "Screamin' Indians" (flying the Sikorsky MH-60S Seahawk), and the HSM-75 "Wolfpack" (with the MH-60R Seahawk).

CVW-11 was part of Carrier Strike Group 11 (CSG-11). In addition to the aforementioned USS *Princeton*, which was one of the *Nimitz*'s escorts (along with the guided-missile destroyers USS *Preble* and USS *Momsen*), CSG-11 was integrated with other ships of the same type, such as the USS *William P. Lawrence* (DDG-110), USS *Stockdale* (DDG-106), USS *Shoup* (DDG-86), and USS *Higgins* (DDG-76).

That was a pretty busy year for CVN-68, which was involved in operations in various locations such as Korea, China, Syria, and Afghanistan. The first of those deployments, during May 2013, saw the *Nimitz* join with the US Navy's 7th Fleet and the South Korean navy in an exercise to face the menace posed by the North Korea regime. That exercise occurred at same time as a similar deployment by the Chinese navy to reaffirm the country's position over the Spratly Islands, then disputed with the Philippines.

The following month saw the commencement of the most important deployment in which the *Nimitz* took part that year: Operation Enduring Freedom in Afghanistan territory, which had been ongoing since 2001. CVW-11 had completed 6,500 flight hours distributed over 1,200 sorties when it left the operational area in August 2013.

In September 2013, the *Nimitz* was readied to launch its aircraft against any potential threat generated by the Syrian regime, amid the controversy about the chemical weapons used in the previous month. However, those weapons were soon put under the UN custody, and the *Nimitz* started to sail back to its home port, Naval Station Everett, Washington, on December 16, 2013, ending an operational year during which CVW-11 aircraft flew over 29,440 flight hours.

For that cruise, the ports of call were Busan, Republic of Korea; Phuket, Thailand; Jebel Ali, United Arab Emirates; Kingdom of Bahrain; Naples, Italy; and Pearl Harbor, Hawaii.

An F/A-18F Super Hornet assigned to the VFA-154 "Black Knights" lands aboard the USS *Nimitz*, then deployed for Operation Enduring Freedom. *US Navy photo by Mass Communication Specialist 2nd Class Jacquelyn D. Childs*

An MH-60R Sea Hawk helicopter assigned to the HSM-75 "Wolf Pack" lifts off from the flight deck of the aircraft carrier USS *Nimitz* during Operation Enduring Freedom. *US Navy photo by Mass Communication Specialist Seaman Derek A. Harkins*

Sailors position an F/A-18E Super Hornet assigned to the "Argonauts" of Strike Fighter Squadron (VFA) 147 onto an elevator aboard the aircraft carrier USS *Nimitz* also during Operation Enduring Freedom. *US Navy photo by MCS3 Raul Moreno Jr.*

US Navy MH-60R Seahawk helicopters assigned to HSM-75 squadron fly past the USS *Nimitz* on June 21, 2013, in the Gulf of Oman during Operation Enduring Freedom. *US Navy photo by Mass Communication Specialist 2nd Class Jason Behnke*

USS *Nimitz* transits the Gulf of Oman during Operation Enduring Freedom. *US Navy photo by MC3 Nathan R. McDonald*

USS *Nimitz* arrives at home port from Operation Enduring Freedom. *US Navy photo by MC1 Nathan Lockwood*

Everett, Washington, December, 2013. Sailors man the rails aboard the USS *Nimitz* as they pull into port at Naval Station Everett. *Nimitz* concluded a deployment supporting Operation Enduring Freedom. *US Navy photo*

Everett, Washington, December, 2013. Sailors man the rails aboard the USS *Nimitz* as they pull into port at Naval Station Everett. *Nimitz* concluded a deployment supporting Operation Enduring Freedom. *US Navy photo*

CHAPTER 5
Sea Trials with the F-35C, Operation Inherent Resolve, and *Nimitz*'s Current Status

In the first days of November 2014, the USS *Nimitz* hosted the sea trials of the naval version of Lockheed Martin F-35 Lightning II fifth-generation fighter. The aircraft successfully performed catapulted take offs and arrested landings, both at day and night.

In early January 2015, CVN-68 entered its Extended Planned Incremental Availability (EPIA) major maintenance cycle, scheduled to last sixteen months. Following the EPIA, the ship went on sea trials in October 2016 to assess its readiness state. Evaluations included the activation of the ship's countermeasure washdown and aqueous-film-forming foam systems, sea-and-anchor and precision anchoring exercises, and ship self-defense weapons, such as the Mk. 38 25 mm machine gun, Mk. 15 Phalanx Close-In Weapons System, and .50-caliber machine guns.

After the positive results from the evaluations, the *Nimitz* joined with destroyers USS *Kidd* (DDG 100) and the aforementioned USS *Shoup*, in addition to other ships to form Carrier Strike Group 11 in early June 2017, amid the tensions generated by the North Korean regime. CSG-11 operated under the 5th and 7th Fleets.

Pacific Ocean, November 4, 2014. Aerial view of two F-35C Lightning II carrier variant joint strike fighters conducts the first catapult launches aboard the USS *Nimitz*. The F-35 Lightning II Pax River Integrated Test Force from Air Test and Evaluation Squadron (VX) 23 is conducting initial at-sea trials aboard *Nimitz*. US Navy photo courtesy of Lockheed Martin by Dane Wiedmann

An F-35C Lightning II carrier variant joint strike fighter prepares to be launched from the USS *Nimitz*. The F-35 Lightning II Pax River Integrated Test Force from Air Test and Evaluation Squadron (VX) 23 is conducting initial at-sea trials aboard *Nimitz*. *US Navy photo courtesy of Lockheed Martin*

An F-35C Lightning II carrier variant joint strike fighters makes an arrested landing aboard the USS *Nimitz*. The F-35 Lightning II Pax River Integrated Test Force from Air Test and Evaluation Squadron (VX) 23 is conducting initial at-sea trials aboard *Nimitz*. *US Navy photo courtesy of Lockheed Martin*

An F-35C Lightning II carrier variant Joint Strike Fighter successfully completes the first carrier launch from the flight deck of the USS *Nimitz*. *US Navy photo by Mass Communication Specialist 3rd Class Huey D. Younger Jr.*

Pacific Ocean, November 6, 2014. An F-35C Lightning II carrier variant joint strike fighter during sea trials aboard the aircraft carrier USS *Nimitz*. *US Navy photo courtesy of Lockheed Martin by Alexander H Groves*

The following month saw the involvement of CVN-68 in Operation Inherent Resolve (OIR) in Syria. For that deployment, CVW-11 kept almost the same units as it had for the previous deployment, but VAW-117 and HSC-6 were replaced by the VAW-121 "Bluetails" and HSC-8 "Eightballers," respectively. The first aircraft launched from USS *Nimitz* for the OIR was an F/A-18E Super Hornet operated by the VFA-147 "Argonauts" in early July, and when the ship's participation for that deployment ended three months later, it had been responsible for 1,322 sorties, during which 1,112 pieces of ordnance were dropped in the US 5th Fleet area of operations.

However, in March 2018, CVN-68 commenced its scheduled Docking Planned Incremental Availability (DPIA). The DPIA comprises multiple modernization works, which will be carried out on a wide range of systems such as steering components, hull preservation, combat systems equipment, aircraft elevator doors, berthing areas, and a new stern dock.

In order to complete the DPIA, the *Nimitz* went from its home port at Naval Base Kitsap to Puget Sound Naval Shipyard and Intermediate Maintenance Facility in Bremerton. The DPIA work ended in April 2019, shortly ahead of the scheduled date and by the time this book went to print the ship was been prepared to enter sea trials

Another photo of the F-35C Lightning II carrier variant joint strike fighter makes an arrested landing conducting sea trials aboard the USS *Nimitz. US Navy photo courtesy of Lockheed Martin by Andy Wolfe*

An F-35C Lightning II carrier variant joint strike fighter lands aboard the USS *Nimitz. US Navy photo courtesy of Lockheed Martin by Andy Wolfe*

Pacific Ocean, November 13, 2014. An F-35C Lightning II carrier variant Joint Strike Fighter conducts its first carrier-based night flight operations aboard the USS *Nimitz*. The aircraft launched at 1801 (PST) and conducted a series of planned touch-and-go landings before making an arrested landing at 1840. *US Navy photo courtesy of Lockheed Martin by Andy Wolfe*

Ships from the *Nimitz* Carrier Strike Group conducting Composite Training Unit Exercise (COMPTUEX) to tests a carrier strike group's mission-readiness and ability to perform as an integrated unit through simulated real-world scenarios, in April 2017. *US Navy photo by Mass Communication Specialist Seaman Ian Kinkead*

The USS *Nimitz* transits through the Arabian Gulf, October 17, 2017, in the Arabian Gulf. *Nimitz* was deployed in the US 5th Fleet area of operations in support of Operation Inherent Resolve. *US Navy photo by Mass Communication Specialist Seaman David Claypool*

Ordnance crew conducts three bombs on the *Nimitz* flight deck. *US Navy*

An F/A-18E Super Hornet stands ready on a flight deck, September 15, 2017, aboard the USS *Nimitz*. *US Air Force courtesy photo by Lt. Col. Alex*

An F/A-18F Super Hornet is launched from the USS *Nimitz* during Operation Inherent Resolve. *US Navy photo by Mass Communication 3rd Class Weston A. Mohr*

Sequence of images depicting the USS *Nimitz* sailing to enter the Docking Planned Incremental Availability (DPIA). *US Navy*

Hundreds of officers and sailors are positioned in various sections of the USS *Nimitz* whilst the vessel departs to the DPIA. *US Navy photo by Mass Communication Specialist 3rd Class Jake Greenberg*

Officers and sailors aligned on deck when the USS *Nimitz* sailed to enter the Docking Planned Incremental Availability (DPIA). *US Navy photo by Mass Communication Specialist 3rd Class Jake Greenberg*

A vision to be kept forever: the USS *Nimitz* sailing calmly. *US Navy photo by Petty Officer 2nd Class Wyatt Anthony*

USS *Nimitz* sailing under the American flag, with hundreds of officers and sailors on deck. *US Navy photo by Mass Communication 3rd Class Cole C. Pielop*

Another photo to mark the beginning of a nine-month dry dock portion of the *Nimitz*'s Docking Planned Incremental Availability maintenance period. *PSNS and IMF photo by Thiep Van Nguyen II*

Puget Sound Naval Shipyard, March 5, 2018. USS *Nimitz* in Dry Dock 6 post dewatering at Puget Sound Naval Shipyard & Intermediate Maintenance Facility in Bremerton, Washington, March 5, 2018. This is the beginning of a nine-month dry dock portion of the *Nimitz*'s Docking Planned Incremental Availability maintenance period. *PSNS and IMF photo by Thiep Van Nguyen II*

USS *Nimitz* in Dry Dock 6 post dewatering at Puget Sound Naval Shipyard & Intermediate Maintenance Facility in Bremerton, Washington, March 5, 2018. *PSNS and IMF photo by Thiep Van Nguyen II*

Another phase of the nine-month dry dock portion of the *Nimitz*'s Docking Planned Incremental Availability maintenance period. *PSNS and IMF photo by Thiep Van Nguyen II*

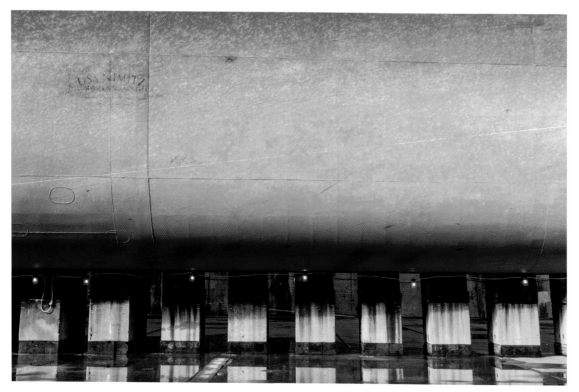

USS *Nimitz* in Dry Dock 6 being submitted to a nine-month dry dock portion of the Nimitz's Docking Planned Incremental Availability maintenance period. *PSNS and IMF photo by Thiep Van Nguyen II*

USS *Nimitz* departed Dry Dock 6 at Puget Sound Naval Shipyard & Intermediate Maintenance Facility in Bremerton, Washington, December 5, 2018. This marked the conclusion of the nine-month dry dock portion of the *Nimitz*'s Docking Planned Incremental Availability maintenance period. *PSNS and IMF photo by Thiep Van Nguyen II*

Another photo to mark the conclusion of the nine-month dry dock portion of the *Nimitz*'s Docking Planned Incremental Availability maintenance period. *PSNS and IMF photo by Thiep Van Nguyen II*

Bibliography

AN/SLQ-32(V) Operator's Handbook.

Bereiter, Gregory. *The US Navy in Operation Enduring Freedom, 2001–2002.* Washington, DC: Naval History & Heritage Command.

Carter, Linwood B. *Iraq: Summary of US Forces.* Washington, DC: CRS Report for Congress, 2005.

Crist, David B. *Joint Special Operations in Support of Earnest Will.* Washington, DC: National Defense University Institute for National Strategic Studies, 2002.

Crowell, Philip H., III. *Innovation and Operation Earnest Will: A Blueprint for Future Low Level Conflicts.* Newport, RI: Naval War College, 1991.

CVN Flight/Hangar Deck NATOPS Manual. Patuxent River, MD: Naval Air Systems Command, 2010.

Friedman, Norman. *US Aircraft Carriers: An Illustrated Design History.* Annapolis, MD: United States Naval Institute, 1983.

Grossnick, Roy A., William J. Armstrong, W. Todd Baker, John M. Elliott, Gwendolyn J. Rich, and Judith A. Walters. *United States Naval Aviation, 1910–1995.* 4th ed. Washington, DC: Naval Historical Center, Department of the Navy, 1997.

Holloway, James L., III, Samuel F. Wilson, Leroy J. Manor, et al. *Special Operations Review Group on the Iranian Hostage Rescue Mission.* Washington, DC: Joint Chiefs of Staff, 1980.

The Hook (Tailhook Association magazine), several issues.

Kelley, Stephen Andrew. *Better Lucky Than Good: Operation Earnest Will as Gunboat Diplomacy.* Monterey, CA: Naval Postgraduate School, 2007.

Landing Signal Officer Reference Manual (REV.B).

Marolda, Edward J. *Ready Sea Power.* Washington, DC: Naval History and Heritage Command, 2012.

Mobley, Richard A. "Fighting Iran: Intelligence Support during Operation Earnest Will, 1987–88." *Studies in Intelligence* 60, no. 3 (Extracts, September 2016).

NATOPS Landing Signal Officer Manual. Washington, DC: Department of the Navy, 2001.

NATOPS Landing Signal Officer Manual. Washington, DC: Department of the Navy, 2009.

Ratner, Steven R. "The Gulf of Sidra Incident of 1981: A Study of the Lawfulness of Peacetime Aerial Engagements." *Yale Journal of International Law* 10, no. 1 (1984): 59–77.

Roe, Charles L. "The NATO Sea Sparrow Surface Missile System." *Johns Hopkins APL Technical Digest* 12, no. 4 (1991).

"Rubber Duck." *Forecast International,* 1997.

"SBROC (Mk. 36)." *Forecast International,* 2000.

"SLQ-25A/B (NIXIE)." *Forecast International,* 2004.

"SPS-49(V)." *Forecast International,* 1999.

"SPS-64(V)." *Forecast International,* 1998.

US Navy Program Guide 2017. Washington, DC: Department of the Navy, 2017.

Walter, R. F. *Free Gyro Imaging IR Sensor in Rolling Airframe Missile Application.* Ft. Belvoir, VA: Ft. Belvoir Defense Technical Information Center, 1999.